The Country Bumpkin Gang

A "Those Were The Days" Book

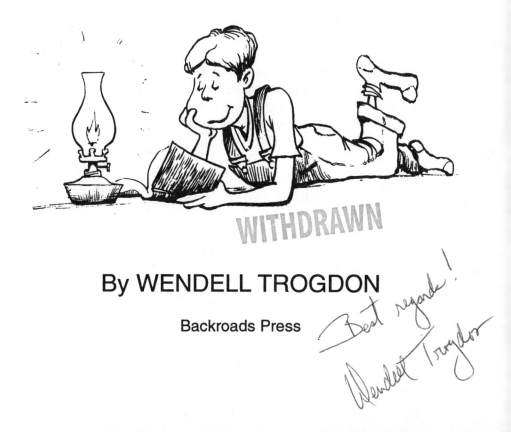

By WENDELL TROGDON

Backroads Press

Best regards!
Wendell Trogdon

Distributed by Wendell Trogdon
and Backroads Press
P.O. Box 651
Mooresville, IN 46158

ISBN 0-9642371-1-3

Cover by Gary Varvel

Printed by
Country Pines Printing
Shoals Indiana

CONTENTS

Dedication

To all those who grew up in rural areas in the 1930s and 1940s. Each may consider himself or herself a member of "The Country Bumpkin Gang."

PART I

Journey Toward Manhood

It was their good fortune, although they would not know it until years later, to be born into hard times.

They were accompanied into life by the Great Depression, an unwanted companion which would stay with them for a decade. It departed only when replaced by a war that would not end until they were in their teens.

It was depression and war, they would realize later, that helped shape their virtues, taught them the value of hard work, increased appreciation of their surroundings and let them know that life can be fragile.

They were country lads who grew up on farms, small plateaus between southern Indiana hills. They lived near Heltonville and Norman, tiny towns where what little social life there was revolved.

They could had they chosen, called themselves "The Country Bumpkin Gang," for others sometimes referred to them as rustics, hillbillies and sodbusters. Those were terms used—perhaps humorously, perhaps insensitively—by city youths to whom the county seat city of Bedford was cosmopolitan.

If the terms bothered the Bumpkins, they did not mind. They sometimes admitted they lived out in the sticks, in areas without electricity where roads were ice covered in winter, coated in mud in the spring, dust in the summer.

They wore bib overalls over bronzed skin when it was warm, their feet bare, toughened by road pebbles, scarred by the hooves of cows and horses. When the temperatures chilled they pulled sock caps over untrained hair, tugged on Mackinaw jackets and protected their hands with double-thumbed gloves that could be reversed when a palm became bare.

Their upstairs bedrooms in rambling, aging farm homes were unheated in winter, uncooled in the summer. A cool drink came from the spring for there was no plumbing, no refrigeration. Radio programs came over console radios, powered by dry cell batteries that often went dead from overuse. What few records they had were played on Victrolas, what live music they heard were songs played and sung by older youths playing fiddles, guitars and banjos.

They watched and played basketball in winter, baseball in the summer. They attended church, lest they miss salvation, feasted at basket dinners, awaited ice cream socials and were uneasy when given roles in Christmas skits.

They watched baptisms in creeks and fidgeted at revivals where the fear of God was preached by evangelists.

They listened and learned from conversations among men at barber shops, general stores and feed mills, picking up words their moms preferred they not use.

At home, they helped with chores, milking cows, feeding livestock, currying horses. By the time they were ten, they had joined men in fields, shucking corn, carrying water to threshing crews, running errands.

Wherever they were, despite the circumstances, they remained upbeat, curious, enthusiastic, eager for whatever awaited them.

Join the "Country Bumpkin Gang" on its journey into manhood and recapture the color, whimsy and integrity of a special time and a special place.

Unappreciated Treasures

Bugsy, Bogey, Tad, Tyke and the others didn't realize in the exuberance of their youth the gems that were in their midst.

The world's jewels, they believed, were out beyond that distant horizon, far from the boundaries of their limited scope. They visualized a dream world where color replaced drabness, places with bright lights instead of coal oil lamps, and excitement that exceeded the routine of farm chores.

Like grass across the fence, life elsewhere was better, or so they imagined. It was a mirage, an illusion like water that seemed to appear in the distance on blacktop roads on a warm day.

Had the innocence of their boyhood not betrayed them, they would have known they lived in a special place and a special time in that era around 1940.

They would have known what an "Historic Sites and Structures Inventory for Lawrence County" would learn five decades later, that the homes they thought were rambling farmhouses were instead landmarks worthy of preservation.

They would not have taunted Ivan about the drafty old brick house where he lived. They would have known it was a two-story "I" house built before the Civil War. They would not have suggested that the old be replaced with the new.

And they would have paid more attention to the place in Zelma where Junior and George lived, a two-story Gothic Revival house built in 1881, they would learn later.

They would have been more impressed had they known the historical importance of two log houses out on the Heltonville-Bartlettsville Road. To them they were "spooky shacks," not reminders of those pioneer days when the land was new. The inventory would cite those homes as two of the township's earliest hewn log houses. One house, the survey learned, dated back to the 1840s.

Tad and Tyke and their friends would have paid more attention when they passed the Norman house on Ind. 58 near the Lawrence-Jackson County line. It looked like just another big old house at the time, not a Greek Revival I-House that would impress preservationists a half century later.

Unaware of architecture, they did not know the Levi Bailey House, built in the 1840s, was an I-house with Greek Revival elements. Or that the columned porticoes out front were part of the original construction.

Barns to Tad and Tyke and the others were different in size and shape and roof, but still barns. They did not know those barns would be what outsiders would call "transverse-frame," "English," "Midwest three-portal."

Bridges, they thought in the 1940s, were to carry traffic, not to be admired. They had no idea they would be labeled later as "Pratt through truss" or "Warren pony truss."

It was a report that would have been wasted on Tad, Tyke, Bugsy and Bogey when they were young. No longer, now that a half-century had passed. Time had shortened their vision, made them more near-sighted.

Places that had been too close to appreciate in their search for the unknown, now seemed significant, reminders of a time that had passed all too quickly. Their eyes had been cast toward the gems in the distance. They had not seen the treasures that had surrounded them.

A Male's Lot

When it came to equal rights there were none on the farm. Not for males, there weren't. And there were no human rights or civil rights organizations to come to their defense.

Bogey's pre-teen friends would not have thought about it had he not raised the issue. He didn't act too smart at times, which is why his associates were surprised when he told them, "Life ain't fair."

Tad, Billy and Tyke had biked with him to Norman that scalding summer afternoon and were cooling off in front of C.E. Cummings' store at Norman.

"Whatta you mean?" Tad asked. He had grown up on a farm between Heltonville and Norman in the depression and hadn't realized that life was better for some than others.

"Well," Bogey said, getting down to basics, "think about chickens. Baby chicks that are female grow up to be pullets, then hens, lay eggs, get fed, housed and cared for as long as they live."

"So what?" Billy asked.

"So what? When the male chicks get to be six to ten weeks old they end up in the fryin' skillet."

"Thank goodness," Tad said. "Ain't nothing better than fried chicken."

That didn't stop Bogey. "Some life! Ten weeks and you end up fried. And something else. How about pigs?"

"How about them?" Tad asked, just to please Bogey.

Bogey replied, "They all end up with rings in their snouts. But female pigs can grow up to be gilts, then sows. Except for a few selected to be boars, males become sexless barrows."

Tad laughed. "Yeah, I helped dad take the hoghood out of some pigs the other day."

Billy was beginning to get Bogey's drift. "And most male horses grow up to be geldings," he said.

"It goes on and on," Bogey interrupted. "Not every male calf grows up to be a rip-snortin' bull. The rest become steers spendin' their lives chewin' on grass, which ain't a bad life, I guess, if you don't have any other interests." He winked to emphasize his point.

"And now," he said, "we have hybrid seed corn that's made possible by taking off tassels—that's the male sex part—on some rows so they won't drop onto the silks—which are the female part. That way the silks can be cross bred from other rows that still have their tassels."

Tyke poured the last of his peanuts into his Coke. "I agree you make a good argument," he said. "But right now, I have to get home to help do the milking."

Bogey said, "That's what I mean. Us guys always have to do the chores. Why can't your sisters do the milking?"

Tyke replied, "Well, I guess they could if they didn't have to wash clothes, gather the eggs, carry water up from the spring, can corn and beans, pick berries and help with the cooking."

As far as work was concerned, both males and females had equal opportunities. Bogey or no Bogey.

Old Fodder Time

To Tad, it was just another winter Saturday. To Jackie, it was as exciting as a circus, better than a Mars bar and a double feature at the theater in Bedford.

Jackie, who lived in Heltonville, never turned down a chance to spend a day in the country.

That's why he had stayed at Tad's home that Friday night in January about 1940, awaiting what he had been told would be a day of corn shredding.

He had never seen a corn shredder, had no idea what one looked like or how one operated.

"Works something like a threshin' machine," Tad, a 12-year-old trying to sound like an expert, told him. "Not many people use a corn shredder any more, now that there are machines which pick off the ears and leave the fodder in the fields.

"That's what we do, but Clem still farms with horses and cuts and shocks his corn in the fall. Then he waits until the ground is frozen so the corn can be brought to the barn lot. And he hires a shredder owner to bring the rig to the farm."

Jackie nodded. Tad continued, "Some folks say Clem is as outdated as the Model T he drives, but Pa says ain't no point in changin' a man's ways as long as he's happy. And Clem seems happy as a calf at suckling time."

Clem was a neighbor who had asked Tad's father and some other farmers to help with the work.

Jackie watched wide-eyed as the shredder lumbered into Clem's barnyard behind a big tractor. Once the machine was backed toward the barn, the tractor was unhooked and turned to face the shredder, a long belt connecting the pulleys of the two machines. A blower pipe was extended into an opening in the barn loft.

The operator engaged the tractor's pulley, causing the belt to turn and the shredder to shudder and shake like a stone crusher. "All set!" the operator yelled.

Tad's dad pulled a load of shocks to the side of the shredder and tossed armloads of eared stalks to the operator who fed them into what looked like a mouth of a monster. The shredder stripped the ears from the fodder, dropping them onto a conveyor which dumped them into a wagon. The stalks were shredded and blown into the barn.

When that load was finished, a second farmer drove up with another one. Tad went with his dad to bring in a third load. Jackie was too fascinated to leave the barn.

The work continued until mid-afternoon when the last load was fed into the shredder. Clem paid the shredder operator, thanked the men who had helped and looked pleased that the job was finished.

"A lot of people, who think fodder has no feed value, call me foolish," he said, "but I reckon this proves I'm not."

He pulled from his bib overall pocket a page torn from the "Farmers Guide" magazine. "Says here that shredded corn fodder is about twice as rich in protein and has about the same level of carbohydrates and fats as oat straw.

"It says," he added with emphasis, "that research shows fodder is more highly regarded than is indicated."

Jackie waited until he and Tad were a few hundred yards away, then said, "He may be outdated, but he isn't dumb. I hope he stays behind the times for another year, so I can watch the corn shredder again."

The Buzz Word

A buzz saw, at the time, didn't seem like something to fear.

Tad and Tyke were in their early teens, young enough to feel immune from harm, old enough to heed the warnings of their father.

It was good there was no Occupational Health and Safety Administration in 1942. Had there been, some families might have had no wood, no warmth at Christmas.

Farm homes around Heltonville had no central heat, only steel barrels converted to stoves or store-bought Warm Mornings.

Tad and Tyke had spent days back in August, in that lull between field work and harvest, helping fill their own wood shed, knowing the work would be easier then than when snow fell and the razor-sharp winds sliced across the hills from the north.

Now it was mid-December, a year after the U.S. had entered World War II. Young men had answered Uncle Sam's call to duty, a few leaving before they could store a winter's supply of wood for their families.

Neither Tad nor Tyke would have complained, even had it not been the Christmas season, when their dad told them he needed their help that Saturday morning. A widow, whose son was in the Army, had bought a load of slabs from a sawmill, he said, adding:

"We'll drive the tractor up there and buzz them."

If their mother was concerned for their safety, she did not complain. A neighbor needed wood and she was proud Tyke and Tad could help cut it. And she knew her husband would caution their sons about the danger they faced.

The buzz saw was mounted on a steel frame that extended out from the front of the Farmall H. A short belt reached from the pulley on the buzz saw to one on the tractor, which when engaged caused the saw to revolve hummingly at hundreds of revolutions per second.

Danger was inches away, and Tad and Tyke knew there would be a lecture before the first slab was cut. Their dad warned them of the hazards, told them they could lose a hand or an arm in the wink of an eye.

At the widow's home, he drove the tractor to the pile of slabs and used a shovel to clear away the snow. "We can't take a chance on slipping when we start the saw," he explained.

He told Tyke, who was 13, two years older than Tad, to "off-bear," which meant he would hold the end of the slab being sawed, then toss it into a pile. "Stand straight, make sure your gloves are on tight and hold the sticks as far to the end as you can," their dad said, adding:

"I'll feed the saw and Tad can hand me the slabs as I need them."

The work went smoothly, the noise deafening any attempt at conversation. The pile of cut pieces grew quickly and the load of slabs was turned to firewood in a few hours.

Tad split some of the wood into small pieces for the woman's kitchen range while Tyke helped his dad do some chores around the barn.

The widow thanked them as best she could.

"Buzzin' wood is dangerous work. I'm grateful to the three of you," she said, cutting them each a quarter of an apple pie.

Tad and Tyke savored the taste. So did their dad.

He held his coffee cup for a refill, then confessed: "I don't want my boys to go through life fearin' things. Besides, I kinda like to cut wood with them. It's one time they pay attention to what I tell them. And they don't act silly doin' it," he said, smiling before taking another bite.

All-American Boy

If Tad's mom had heard it once, she had heard it a 100 times. Monday through Friday she heard it, almost as soon as Tad hurried into the house, tossed aside his books and turned on the battery-powered radio.

The words never changed, not at 5 p.m., or was it 5:15 p.m., around 1940:

"Wheaties, the breakfast of champions, brings you the exciting adventures of Jack Armstrong, the all-American boy."

It was a prelude to 15 minutes of exemplary conduct for the hero of Hudson High, a school that could have been in any city or town in America. Jack wasn't a farm boy like Tad and his buddies. No matter. He had a sense of adventure, just like they did.

Tad didn't move once he plopped beside the console. He just nodded a thank you when his mom brought him the sugar cookies fresh from the oven of the wood range in the kitchen.

He sat through the Hudson High fight song, "Wave the flag for Hudson High, boys, show them how we stand. Ever shall our team be champions, known throughout the land."

It was no wonder Tad had Wheaties, with thick cream, every morning. Not after his daily indoctrination:

"Have you tried Wheaties?

"They're whole wheat with all of the bran.

"Won't you try Wheaties?

"For wheat is the best breakfast food in the land."

His mom didn't argue about the health benefits of Wheaties. She did wonder why he just sat, listening, listlessly. "Your ear will grow to that radio," she warned him more than once. "Wouldn't you rather do your chores now, instead of later?"

If Tad heard her, he didn't react. He just kept listening to the adventures of his airwaves hero. The only part of him that moved was his right hand, that only slightly when he wrote the information needed to order a Jack Armstrong gadget for "just one Wheaties box top and a dime."

Gadgets were useful on weekends, gadgets like a Jack Armstrong whistle which let him signal his buddy, Ray, who lived up the gravel road. Two whistles meant, "Meet me at once. I have some big news."

Tad's mom never went to the store without his reminder, "Don't forget the Wheaties?"

Tad listened through November, December, January, February and into March, almost always putting off his chores until the program was over.

That changed, though, when the temperatures warmed the days grew longer and the grass greened.

Not even Jack Armstrong could keep Tad indoors. Real life adventures awaited him in the theater of the outdoors.

Mad Money

Tad and Tyke looked up from their hoes and waved as their friends rode past the field on their bikes that June afternoon.

Bugsy, Billy and Bogey didn't stop as they pedalled south toward Back Creek and the swimming hole. Tad and Tyke, they knew, had shoots to chop from the corn, that for them work came before fun. It was a warm day and a dip in the cool water would be refreshing, but it would have to wait for Tad and Tyke.

Chances are their dad wouldn't have cleared the trees and the brush from the land and turned it into what he called "new ground" had he not had his sons to help.

World War II was underway and the extra acreage would produce a crop that might, in a small way, help feed a nation and secure a victory. Now, the corn grew, dark green and healthy. So did the sassafras, maple and oak shoots emerging from roots which remained alive in the soil.

It was the job of Tad, Tyke and Jimmy, the hired hand, to clear that growth from between the stalks. Jimmy knew Tad and Tyke would prefer to relax between dips in the cool water pooled in the creek than remain in the field. He also knew that life wasn't easy. His certainly hadn't been.

He opened a window to his soul, explained to the boys that the constitution did not extend them freedom from effort, that little is gained without labor, that joy can come from work well done. Jimmy talked as he hoed, working quickly, trying to keep up with his shadow as he headed east across the field.

"Your reward will come. Just wait," he told them, stooping over to pick up an arrowhead left by a departed people who, too, had lived off the land.

Tad and Tyke worked and listened, knowing Jimmy was probably right, but still upset that they had to work while others played. In the distance, they could see their dad, high on the seat of the Farmall, cultivating corn in an older field, too far away to read the discontent in their faces.

The work continued until Saturday afternoon. Tad and Tyke headed for the creek after lunch, spending the afternoon alone as they looked forward to a night in Norman where a free movie would be shown on the side of C. E. Cummings' store.

They had no money except what was in their bank accounts, not even a nickel for a soft drink. That changed when their dad called them into the living room after supper.

He had been as tough as sirloin of bull when he expected them to work, now he was as easy as cream of wheat. He handed each of them a $1 bill, thanked them for a week's work, indicated he was pleased with what they had done.

They joined Bugsy, Billy and Bogey at Norman that night, walking among the crowd which spilled onto Ind. 58.

"Let's stop for a triple-dip ice cream cone," Tad suggested.

Bugsy shook his head. "Just spent my last nickel for a Pepsi. Billy and Bogey are broke, too."

This time, Bugsy, Bogey and Billy watched as Tad and Tyke savored the reward of their new ground labor which had put money in their pockets.

Green As Gourds

Gourds didn't always get the respect they deserved. Witness: "He's out of his gourd." Or, "He's as green as a gourd." Or, "He's a gourd head."

* * *

Bugsy pointed to a pump outside an abandoned house and hurried toward it. Tad saw the pump, too. His eyes brightened like he had spotted an oasis in the desert.

It was a cool November day in the late 1930s, but the nine-year-old boys wrapped in warm clothing had worked up a thirst exploring the hills and hollows northeast of Heltonville.

Chances are, they knew, there would be no dipper, but they could cup their hands and drink from the spout.

Bugsy reached the pump first and worked the handle up and down, then checked the water to make sure it looked clean and smelled pure. He hadn't noticed the dipper that dangled on a wire on the pump.

Tad removed the cup, held the long handle in his right hand and sipped the water. He wiped his mouth with his coat sleeve and handed the dipper to Bugsy.

"That's better," Bugsy said as he finished a long drink, his thirst quenched. He turned the dipper in his hand, eying it closely, curiously.

"It's made from a gourd," Tad explained. "Someone hollowed out the inside of the bowl, left the rest to form the handle, then used a piece of wire to hang the cup from the pump. It's a good thing it's a gourd cup. A tin cup would be rusted by now 'cause no one has lived here for a couple of years."

The boys returned to their homes. Tad told his mom about the gourd dipper.

"People have used gourds for generations, maybe centuries," she said, explaining different-shaped gourds could be used for all sorts of things. "Things," she said, "like bottles, flower pots, flour or sugar scoops, ladles and bowls."

She had made some of those items herself. "You just take the fruit out of the shells, then let the shells dry," she explained.

Tad forgot about gourds until he recalled, the next week at school, the one on the pump. He stopped at the library at recess pulled out the "G" encyclopedia and opened it to "gourd."

One sentence caught his eye. ". . . for primitive people without either metalware or pottery, gourds may be used for cutlery, utensil scoops, ladles, fish net floats, whistles and rattles."

His mom laughed that night when he asked, "Are people who make things out of gourds primitive?"

"Just poor," she replied.

He would ask his dad later to show him how to make a whistle from a dried gourd.

Dullsville It Wasn't

Ken didn't do much work, living in Bedford as he did, except maybe mow the yard when he couldn't get out of it.

His arms weren't bronzed from days in the sun and he still had the fat he'd gathered sitting in the classroom the past school year.

He seemed to consider himself a step above his country cousins, appeared to think their lives in those early days of the 1940s were dull, uneventful. He liked to taunt Chig, another pre-teen he knew from occasional visits to the rural church his parents sometimes attended.

"Must be exciting watching corn grow," he teased Chig, not even bothering to plant tongue in cheek before adding: "What do you do for excitement, walk up and down the hills on stilts? Maybe watch moles burrow in the yard?"

Chig would have straightened him out with a punch to his inflated midsection had they not been in full view of Saturday shoppers on the Courthouse Square in Bedford.

Ken kept up his banter. "Suppose you'll be going to bed with the chickens tonight." Chig laughed, despite his anger.

"Nope! Tonight is the free show at Norman. Three, maybe, four hundred people will be there."

Ken snorted. "It'll probably be some old silent picture that won't be any good."

Chig shook his head. "We got talkies now. Anyhow, if the movie is not any good, I can walk up and down the streets and talk with kids who come into town from miles around."

"So you got something to do one night of the week," Ken shrugged.

"Guess you don't know about the basket dinner at church tomorrow. There'll be tables filled with good stuff like chocolate cake, apple pie, banana pudding and enough cookies to fill my pants pockets. Mom's already said I could skip the afternoon preachin' and play across the road in Charley Mark's woods."

Ken smirked, "Big deal. So it's one weekend of the summer."

Chig continued to outline his social schedule. "Lots of other things coming up, too. There's an ice cream social at church Thursday night. Next week, I'll start carrying water for the threshing machine crew, which means we'll have big dinners every day for at least two weeks. May even get to ride in a truck taking wheat over to the Bundy Brothers elevator in Medora."

Ken didn't interrupt. Chig continued: "After that, there's the Jackson County Fair over at Brownstown. I'll go there a couple of days, spend all my money at the carnival the first day, then look over the animals and exhibits the second day. "Watermelons will be ripe by then, so me and dad will make at least two trips over to the Vallonia bottoms to pick up all we can get in the car.

"And when I get a chance, 'Buck' says I can ride with him up to Indianapolis when he takes a truck load of livestock to market."

It was almost enough to impress even a city boy.

Ken looked at Chig and said, "I wouldn't want to be in your shoes. You must never have time not to do anything."

This time he had his tongue in cheek, or so it looked to Chig.

Food For Thought

Bugsy had an appetite that was bigger than the farm where he lived.

Eggs, bacon or sausage, home-made hot biscuits and gravy and oatmeal weren't enough for breakfast. He had to top them off with cold cereal.

He'd shake out a bowl from a box, add a coating of sugar, if World War II rationing allowed, and top it off with cream from the separator.

Sometimes he might ask for hot Cream of Wheat, but it really wasn't a man's meal, being advertised as it were by a girl, even if she was Shirley Temple.

"I've seen threshing machines that didn't devour as much fiber as you," his dad taunted him.

Bugsy was still a pre-teen and his mother considered him a growing boy who needed fuel to run until noon.

His dad moaned about the cost of the cereal, which had to be bought at the store, unlike most food that was on the kitchen table. Bugsy explained its educational value with the vigor of a salesman trying to convince a reluctant shopper. He turned a box of Wheaties in his hands, pointing to the literature on the sides.

"Reading material," he said between bites. "Gives me something to keep my mind sharp, now that school is out."

"And boxtop to order all those rings, pedometers or whatever Jack Armstrong offers on the radio this week," his dad responded.

Bugsy nodded and read from the box: "Attention girls! (this being the 1940s when women were called girls). Here comes the real Head Man." The words appeared amid a drawing of a farmer, a rooster and four hens. He read on:

"Yes, you are in command of one of Uncle Sam's most important production units. And here's your first order of the day—to make sure you and your family get the good, nourishing breakfast hard working Americans need every morning. So start

47441

that first meal in champion style with plenty of milk and fruit and Wheaties—Breakfast of Champions."

Bugsy would switch the next morning to Post Toasties for new reading material. A father appeared on that box with his wife and two children, exclaiming, "What a break! A swell-tasting breakfast that helps to give us the Vitamin B1, we need daily."

Bugsy scanned the box. "Post Toasties now give you this precious energy vitamin—and it's in no other corn flakes. An extra benefit—at no extra cost?"

He looked up at his Mom. "Let's get Kellogg's Corn Flakes the next time. The flakes are bigger and they taste better than Post Toasties."

She added, "And you haven't read what's on the new Kellogg boxes."

"Hope it's more than what's on Cream of Wheat," he said, reciting the Cream of Wheat jingle:

"Little Indian, Sioux or Crow,
"Little Frosty Eskimo,
"Little Turk or Japanee,
"Oh don't you wish that you were me?
"You have curious things to eat
"I am fed on—Cream of Wheat."

His mother wrote his request on the lined note pad she kept as a reminder of what she wanted in town.

"Need to get rolled oats, too," she said. "I read where Quaker Oats are putting cups in its boxes."

His dad opened another biscuit and covered it with sausage gravy. He had been boxed in. "I'll be glad when school starts," he muttered. "Textbooks are cheaper than cereal boxes and what comes with them."

Bugsy corralled the last flake in his bowl, stood up and tried to locate any muscle in his right arm. Only a cereal box and its content could improve a boy's brain and brawn at one sitting.

Or let his mother obtain a new setting of cups.

Lasting Scars

It was all but impossible for a boy to grow up in the hill country without scars on his hands, arms and knees.

The marks of boyhood came from bike wrecks, bodies hurdling over handlebars onto gravel roads while riding lickety-split down steep hills. Reminders of accidents, like brands on horses brought in from the west, would remain with them forever.

Kids in town could ride on smooth tarvy or concrete. Boys in the country had to pedal over county roads to reach blacktop highways. Bugsy was no exception. He lived on a farm east of Heltonville, down on Back Creek Road, "Possum Holler Road" some visitors called it.

Bugsy hadn't had his bike long. Just since his check came from the stockyards, paying him for the hog his dad had given him. The bicycle was still new, unscratched; still shining red, the Western Flyer emblem still glistening.

Bugsy was younger than most of his farm buddies that spring, 1941 or 1942 he recollects. He had learned to ride on the paths in the pastures and he was ready to expand his horizon by the time the winter moisture dried from the thinly graveled roadways.

Cars and trucks had worn two grooves into the one-lane road, kicking gravel out to the edges. He pedaled easily in one track, his buddy Chig beside him in the other groove. He was excited, eager to ride the three miles or so down to U.S. 50.

He had paid little heed when he noticed Chig had rolled his right pant leg halfway to his knee. The boys coasted down the steep hill, started pedaling again at Saul Barrett's house and panted their way up a steeper hill. Chig darted to the left, Bugsy to the right as a car approached at the crest of the hill.

Bugsy stopped, just inches from a cliff at the side of the road, looking down toward a creek where he might have ended up if he had not been careful. They listened more closely for cars at the next hill, then relaxed as the road flattened out in the Back Creek bottoms.

At U.S. 50 they reversed directions and started back toward home. Bugsy was getting the hang of the road. He raced down the first hill and was planning to descend the next even more quickly. Halfway down, his pant leg caught in the chain, flipping him off the bike that clung to him as he sprawled in the gravel.

His left palm was a mass of bruises, his wrist was coated with stone dust reddened by blood, the knees of his overalls were torn, and his kneecaps skinned.

Chig turned the pedals of the bike, freeing Bugsy's pant leg. He helped his injured friend stand and examine the bike.

They straightened the goose neck which had been twisted awry. The bike no longer was new. A fender was bent, the paint was scarred. It had been introduced to life in the country.

Bugsy returned home to his mom's first aid kit, tried to rub out the scratches on his bike, wiped the dust from the frame and from the spokes.

He rode again the next day, but not until he had rolled up his pant leg. Later he would buy metal clamps that kept his pant leg from catching in the chain at the sprocket.

But he would have other accidents on his Western Flyer. And each new scar would be a reminder of the spills, the upsets, the crashes, the turnovers on the roadway of life.

It Was So Hot

Bugsy earned $1.50 a day working on a hay baler that summer of '43, which gave him an air of confidence and independence.

He was 13, going on 31, thanks to being around grown men so much. He had taken on the demeanor of manhood, spitting and spicing his conversations with swear words, offering opinions on almost any topic of the day.

Hours under the sun had darkened his skin, bleached his hair and made him immune to the heat of summer.

Reading the paper kept his mind sharp. All of which helps explain why Bugsy reacted as he did one night as he waited outside the church near Heltonville for the revival meeting to start. He was surrounded by Freddie and three or four other lads, none older than eight.

"Sure hate to go inside," one of them said, trying to impress Bugsy. "It'll be hotter than hell in there."

Another said, "This must be the hottest summer we've ever had." Bugsy, himself, couldn't have scripted a better line for his entrance into the exchange.

"You guys are all too young to remember back in the summer of '36. I was just a boy myself then, but I tell you if there is a hell, I lived through it."

"Well, how hot was it?" one of the boys asked. Bugsy said, "Hot enough for the tarvy to ooze like jelly out of the pavement on Ind. 58. Hot enough for the bull to run in the opposite direction when a neighbor brought a heifer to be serviced."

Freddie asked it the temperature went above 100.

"You gotta be kiddin'," Bugsy said, pleased to be the center of attention. "A hundred was a cold wave. It was 108 in late June, 104 right after the Fourth of July. Then it turned warm. By July 25, we had 10 days straight when it was 100 degrees or higher and it was 110 three different days."

One of his listeners wanted to know what he did to keep cool. It was like asking the evangelist about sin.

"Tried to forget about how hot it was. We'd wallow like hogs in the swimmin' hole until the water got too warm, then see how few clothes we could wear and still be decent.

"Not having any electricity for refrigeration there was nothing cold to drink except water from the spring. Dad tried to bring some ice home from Bedford one day, but most of it melted before he got out of the city limits.

"I'd sleep out on the porch most nights because my upstairs bedroom under the tin roof was hot as an oven. I'd have gone to a cave, like some people did, but I didn't have any way to get there except on my bike and it was too hot to ride it."

The bell rang for the revival meeting to start. Bugsy passed up the fans that were being handed out. "After what I went through back in '36, I won't need that," he said.

On the way home that night, Freddie said, "That Bugsy sure is a windjammer. He was tellin' us that it was way hotter in 1936 than it is now. Said it was above 100 a lot of days and 110 sometimes."

His dad laughed. "Bugsy may like to talk, but he's right about that summer in '36. Chances are he read the same newspaper story about that summer as I did the other day. It was a summer I'll never forget even without newspapers to remind me. Why, it was so hot . . ."

Bugsy pulled a comic book from the pocket on the back of the front seat of the car and fanned himself. "I've already heard this story once tonight," he thought to himself.

Cabin Fever Cure

Winter darkness had turned to spring bright. Nature was in the midst of repainting winter drab with awakening green. A season of lethargy was surrendering to a bustle of activity.

It was a good time to be alive for men and boys, for mothers and daughters, for farm animals and wildlife great and small.

Had Chig been older, he might have paid more attention to that special time in late March, 1942, made some notes to remember all the details. But he was too wrapped up in the mysteries of life that surrounded him.

Written reminders or not, he would remember much of what he observed that day. Things like:

*His dad feeling his oats, literally, on a sunny Saturday. Chig had helped, poured the oats from the seed sack into the drill box, unbagged the 2-12-6 bags of Buhner Happy Farmer fertilizer.

He had ridden on the drawbar of the Farmall as his dad pulled the drill.

His dad hadn't looked happier since he cribbed the last load of corn last November. A new growing season was alive to give purpose to his role as a farmer.

Oats was a good crop, he told Chig. "You can sow a crop in late March and harvest it in July and let the clover seed we're drilling with it keep growing for a hay crop."

*His mom and sister, too, were caught up in the enthusiasm of spring. They were cleaning house, a room at a time, moving furniture outside to refresh itself in the sun. They took turns whacking the dust out of rugs draped over the clothes lines.

They were chores Chig wanted to avoid, so he remained in the field, except when he climbed the rail fence to walk into the woods. The softwood trees already were beginning to show traces of leaves, wildflowers facing the sun were in bloom, mayapple plants were pushing aside the leaves that had been their winter blanket.

*Out on the gravel road, there was more traffic than usual. Families who had spent the winters fighting colds and cabin fever were on their way to town.

The mud had already disappeared from the road, the thaw was over and their cars stirred up clay dust, reddened by the sun.

Had it not been for a gnawing hunger, Chig would have stayed in the field through the dinner hour. He paid for his ham and bean lunch by helping return to the house the furniture his mom and sisters had removed.

He noted his dad's expression change as he scanned the newspaper the mail carrier had left, saw a frown replace a smile. Chig would learn later that what saddened his dad was a news story about the valiant defense American-Filipino troops had fought against the Japanese on the Bataan peninsula before surrendering.

It would be the only sadness in a day of joy that would be worth remembering.

PART II

Age of Innocence

The "Country Bumpkins" seldom engaged in malicious mischief, there being few avenues to trouble. Oh, they smoked corn silks, tried cigarettes, tested home brew and perpetrated pranks at Halloween.

Marijuana was not a problem. Cocaine, heroin, crack were words in the dictionary; psychedelic drugs were two decades in the future.

Except for basketball games and Saturday nights, they went to bed early, knowing the time for morning chores would arrive before their desire to perform them.

Their greatest vices may have been the exaggeration of some of their stories. Gordie, for example, had an imagination to match his enthusiasm. Once on a roll, he shifted into overdrive, turning a routine experience into a drama worthy of a Saturday Evening Post feature.

They read sports pages and comic books, paid attention to Charles Atlas body building advertisements, and sneaked looks at their big sisters' romance magazines.

Few strangers traveled the narrow roads where the "Bumpkins" lived. Those who did were greeted as friends by youngsters eager to learn from those who came from different backgrounds with stories they had not before heard.

Hoboes with knapsacks sometimes left the box cars on the Milwaukee, St. Paul and Chicago tracks to seek out food at farm houses. Few families turned them away. Some wives, big of heart and tender of soul, packed food for them after sharing their dinner table.

Junk men came, seeking bargains in steel, zinc or other metals tossed onto scrap heaps. A huckster wagon arrived once each week, the driver accepting eggs in trade for staples. A middleman, driving a pickup truck, showed up twice a week, picking up cream and cubed home-made butter from the spring. The income gave mothers cash to stow in pitchers in the corner cupboard.

It was, perhaps, the isolation of their lives that allowed Tad, Bugsy and their friends to be aware of people and things, to store in the recesses of the mind stories that would rerun forever in the theaters of their memories.

Hoboes and Junk Men

March brought more than a new season to isolated areas around Heltonville. It was accompanied by visitors who arrived when the seasons changed, the frost left the ground and south winds warmed the air.

Bugsy and his friends remember their visits. Consider the stories they tell a half-century later.

Bugsy recalls that hoboes hopped off the freight trains on the Milwaukee tracks as they slowed down for the Ind. 58 crossings. The homeless men walked through fields and down gravel roads, going house to house begging for food.

"Tramps, Dad called them," Bugsy remembers. "Mom said they were just down on their luck. We still had enough stuff in the cellar to last another three winters, so Dad didn't complain when she fed them."

Tyke remembered those hoboes. "Dad, one time, agreed to feed a tramp supper and breakfast and let him sleep in the barn if he'd help build fence the next day.

"The tramp agreed. He had three helpings of ham and beans at supper, four eggs, three sausages and more biscuits than I could count for breakfast. When Dad went to get the post hole diggers out of the shed, the tramp took off up the road like a man being chased by hard work. He got two meals and a bed in the hay free without working a lick. All Dad got in return was something to fuss about the rest of the day."

He got off easy compared to Chig's father. "These three guys in a mud covered Model A truck drive into our barn lot and offer to paint the barn roof for $50," Chig relates.

"Dad says, 'That sounds like a fair price' and the men use big brushes to spread the stuff over the galvanized sheets. Dad looks at the roof and says, 'Looks good,' and wrote out a check. About two days later, it rained for hours. You should have heard Dad when he saw the downpour had washed off whatever it was the men had put on the roof. The only thing left was this oily stuff on the ground instead of on the tin."

Tad remembers the junk man who stopped by the farm one day. "My parents had gone to town. 'Any junk?' the guy said. I sold him some zinc from can lids and a few other things I'd been saving. He offered me a dollar for an old harrow and I took it.

"I gave Dad the dollar when he got home and he hit the ceiling. Said just because the harrow was a little rusty didn't mean it wasn't any good. He took off, caught up with that ol' junk man and paid him $5 to get that harrow back."

Larry had stories about the Watkins man who sold everything from vanilla extract to petro-carbo salve which he said would cure anything from saddle gall to minor cuts.

Bob said his mother was always happy to see the door-to-door knife sharpener. "Dad tried to sharpen them like he did a scythe and that always made them worse."

But it was Pokey who had the best story about a spring visitor.

"Pa had skinned his hands when he was puttin' new points on the plow and was cussin' like he did when things weren't goin' well. He looked up at this guy in a shirt and tie and asks, 'What the hell do you want?'

"The man bites his lip to keep from laughin'. 'I'm the new preacher,' he says. The preacher and Dad shook hands and became friends for life."

After all it was spring, a time to start anew.

A Generation Apart

Pot, as far as most country boys knew, was a granite container their moms used to make coffee. It certainly was not, to their limited teen-age experiences of the early 1940s, a drug to be smoked.

They seldom dared buy Marvels for eight cents a pack or Camels which cost a dime. Cigarettes, their parents and their coaches warned, would harm their bodies, stunt their growth and limit their stamina.

"Evil," some fundamentalist ministers around Heltonville said of cigarettes.

No teen, at least those who associated with Chig, Tyke, Bugsy and their buddies, lighted a smoke in sight of an adult. And marijuana was a word to which they did not relate.

They grew toward manhood, consumed by the trials of adolescence, ever alert to the news that unfolded on the World War II battlefields around the world.

Older teens they knew went to war as soon as they reached 17 or 18. They had little time to loaf or be idle as had jobless young men of the depression years of the 1930s.

It was just as well. Older adults with time on their hands might have exposed their younger neighbors to new experiences. Instead Chig and his friends remained free of any temptation they might, otherwise, have had.

It would be years later before they knew that pot, even cocaine, had been available in that earlier decade. It was news to them when they finally learned that marijuana was a drug of the depression, that 50 tons of the weed had been destroyed in Indiana as early as 1938. Or that smoking pot was on the increase in the years before America went to war and galvanized an entire generation in a united effort.

The teens of the 40s had been too young to attend that midnight show at the Indiana Theater in Bedford when a movie news reel called marijuana "the weed with roots in hell." They had turned to the comics and sports page in 1939, missing the news item that a marijuana plant had been found in Lawrence County.

Their parents had taken the "Farmer's Guide," not the "Prairie Farmer," which had campaigned against marijuana. They had not yet read a history of Lawrence County, which reported a 1930s warning: "Dreaded opium is merely a sedative, compared to the danger of marijuana. Armies have been crazed and countless lives lost and debauched through its devastating effect on the brain."

The history book recorded that "The Mexican weed" or "India Hemp" was used among college students more than others in the 1930s. It was of no concern to Bugsy, Chig and Tyke and their friends, this belated knowledge of a decade that preceded their adolescence. They had never missed what they didn't know existed.

Ignorance was not a virtue, they decided, but neither had it been a vice.

As they grew older "pot" did take on a new meaning for them. Not as in marijuana, but as in the money on the table in friendly poker games.

* * * *

Postscript: When marijuana resurfaced again in the 1960s some people called it "a new threat." It may have been a threat, but it was not new.

This Bud For Brew

Had there been a mold for the exemplary teen, it wouldn't have fit Bud. He preferred to live beyond the limits most parents set for their sons.

That doesn't mean he was a bad sort, for he wasn't. But he did like to challenge life rather than submit to it. He tested authority, dared to do what others were frightened to do, stretched boldness to its limits.

Take that warmer-than-normal winter night in the mid-1940s. Bud, who was barely 16, had driven his Model A into Heltonville in search of excitement. He found none, which wasn't unusual.

He did, however, locate three friends, all younger than he, which may have been why they were impressed with the tales he spun. He entertained them for a half hour or so, licked his lips and said, "A beer would taste good right now."

The others thought it was an empty wish, there being no tavern in Heltonville and Bud being too young to enter had there been one. "Where you gonna get a beer?" Tyke asked.

"Get in," Bud said. All three did, lest they be ridiculed. Tad wondered where he was headed.

"Out home," he said. "Dad makes home brew and he has some in the cellar under the house."

Tyke was skeptical. "And he's going to let you have some of it!"

Bud laughed. "Yeah! Like he's going to give me a $25-a-week allowance. He'd kill me if he knew I was going to sneak it out of the house. But he'll be asleep and I can find the beer without turning on a single light."

Tad, Tyke and Jake waited in the car while Bud tip-toed around the house, then eased himself down the steps to the cellar. He returned with three Mason jars cradled in his arms. "Told you," he said, as he let the car roll down an incline lest its start awaken his parents.

He stopped a mile or two away, unscrewed the zinc lid and lifted a jar to his lips. "Good stuff," he said, handing the jar to Tyke, who didn't share his opinion of the taste. Neither did Tad or Jake.

They had barely finished the first jar when Tyke said he needed to get home lest his folks send out a search party. Tad and Jake concurred. Bud laid the two unopened jars in the seat beside him.

He would confess to the others later that he had returned them to the cellar that night. His father, he knew, might miss three jars, but not one. And he was smart enough not to try the home brew heist again. It was more challenging to come up with a new stunt.

* * *

Bud died in 1992. He outgrew his need for bedevilment, but he never fit into the mold of the self-righteous. He was, however, a veteran who served his country, a man who had worked hard, raised a family, did good. Bartenders at a lodge in Bedford kept the seat he preferred empty, an open beer at his place at the bar, until after the funeral.

His dad would have been proud of him, even if he had known about that night a half century ago.

Moe, Joe and Dough

Moe and Joe lived with their parents a half-mile or so off a county road between Heltonville and Norman.

Moe and Joe weren't their real names. They are called that, lest they take offense, whereever they may be. It is doubtful if they would for they were not vindictive types.

Their folks had no car, couldn't afford one, had no need to sprinkle gravel on the narrow lane which meandered to the house. Their dad had no steady winter job, seldom found work except when someone needed help butchering hogs or cutting wood.

What money he made went to keep a roof on the little rough lumber house and buy enough groceries to keep food on the table and put bologna between bread for the lunch Moe and Joe carried to school at Heltonville.

By mid-March, inlaid cardboard could be seen through the soles of the boys' shoes when they crossed their legs at the patches which covered their knees. Broken, oft-spliced laces, had been replaced with binder twine.

They had but one pair of faded overalls each, which grew more mud coated each day of the week. Their mother washed them on weekends, but not on weekdays. The heavy blue denim wouldn't have dried overnight, even if draped over a chair next to the wood heating stove.

Their hair had grown longer each week, becoming more entangled under the sock caps they wore to keep their heads warm on their walks to and from the bus. A curry comb, it appeared, would have been needed to part their hair.

Neither Joe nor Moe ever complained about the teasing they sometimes endured from others who weren't much better groomed themselves. Like their dad, they had no pretense; had been taught that character outweighed appearance. And they knew their friends razzed students they liked and ignored those they didn't like well.

Teachers, to their credit, paid little attention to how Moe and Joe looked. Both made good grades, even if they had to do their homework next to kerosene lamps.

All that didn't mean Joe and Moe wouldn't have preferred new clothes and monthly haircuts. It meant they could survive without them.

Warm, bright days arrived at last to wash away the grime of winter, repaint the hills and fields, transform the landscape, dry the moisture from the dirt lane.

Spring changed Moe and Joe even more. It was a Saturday morning in early April when they walked out of the barber shop, their hair cut, parted neatly with Brilliantine oil.

They had smiles as wide as the Heltonville town limit sign. Their dad trailed behind. "Takin' them to Bedford to get new shoes and new overalls," he said, "so they'll have something new to wear the last two weeks of school."

No one at school was better dressed, cleaner, neater that next Monday. No one asked about the change in Moe and Joe and neither said anything until they were on the bus home.

Joe let his friends know their dad had been hired as a field hand by a farmer, at least through the planting season. Moe, the quieter of the two, said, "It's too bad we don't go to school in the summer now that we have new clothes and the lane isn't muddy."

He laughed, so none would think he was serious. No matter. Moe and Joe had survived another winter. And they would survive similar winters to come.

They eventually moved. Even though they weren't heard from again, they're still remembered . . . and will be as long as spring follows winter.

The Smoke Out

Buddy was more of a braggart than an achiever, which explains why he was a year or two older than his junior high companions.

He talked a better game than he played, but no one seemed to mind once they recognized his talk exceeded his deeds.

Well, at least one teacher did mind. She had held him back a grade.

But that didn't make him a bad sort. He could be tolerated, once it was realized his pretense was more veil than vanity.

Actually he had the same fears, the same self-doubts as any other junior high school student at Heltonville.

That was never more obvious than one February night in 1942 when he walked toward home after a basketball game. His best buddy, Froggie, was with him. So were Tad and Tyke, Bob and Billy, who lived on farms east of town.

They talked about the game, agreed Heltonville would have won had Boob Henderson not been hurt, and complained about the officiating as usual.

But the conversation turned to "The War" as it always did, sooner or later, that dark winter of uncertainty and wonder.

They talked about rationing that was to come, civil defense measures, air raid wardens, lookout posts where volunteers would be assigned to search the skies for enemy planes.

And finally they mentioned the blackouts that were ordered from time to time to turn the nation into a sea of darkness in case Axis bombers penetrated the coastal defenses looking for targets.

Bob said his folks pulled the blinds to shield the lights. "We just blow out the kerosene lamps," said Tad who lived beyond the reach of electric lines.

Buddy laughed at their alarm. "Ain't gonna be no planes attackin' us. Not this far inland, anyhow," he said. "I ain't scared of no German nor no Jap," he said, adding, "Just four years separate me from gettin' at those guys."

He pulled a cigarette from the eight-cent pack of Marvels he carried in his shirt pocket, tugged a kitchen match from his pocket, struck it with his right thumb nail. The tip of the lighted cigarette glowed in the darkness as they walked along Ind. 58.

"So much for tonight's blackout," Billy moaned. "As dark as it is, that Marvel can be seen for miles."

Buddy snickered in defiance. But only for a moment. Maybe it was coincidence or fate, but a "huummmmmm" sliced through the stillness of the cool night air.

"It's a plane." said Tyke. "Could be a German bomber!" The others, except for Buddy, knew he was kidding.

Buddy was suddenly silent. The boys walked on for a hundred yards or so before running steps overtook them. "Had to stop back there a minute," Buddy explained, like maybe he had to relieve himself.

It was another half mile before he reached home, but he didn't light up another cigarette. He pulled Tyke to his side before he went into the house, handed him the rest of the cigarettes, and said, "Get rid of these for me. And if Mom asks you later what happened to my clothes, tell her we got into a friendly little scuffle."

Tyke asked, "What for?"

Buddy whispered, "I don't want her to know I had the cigarettes. Or that I put one out and tore my pants when I jumped into a ditch after Tyke said that plane might be a German bomber."

A Day In May

Bugsy had whined that morning, moaning that he couldn't listen to the 500-Mile Race if he was helping his dad in the field. His protest fell on deaf ears.

It was May 30, 1941, a Friday. Rain had delayed seeding soybeans in the last field and his dad told him the work could not be delayed, not even for the big race up at Indianapolis.

"You can read about it tomorrow," his dad said. "And you can read today's paper when you aren't busy."

Bugsy's job was to inoculate the soybean seed to make sure it would germinate. To do that he had to dump the beans into a tub, then stir the black inoculant in an effort to coat each seed.

That didn't take much time, not for a 12-year-old boy, who didn't make work last any longer than necessary. He squinted in the sun as he read the newspaper his dad placed in the wagon. He read about the sinking of the Bismarck . . . and noted the date of the paper.

He turned to the sports pages and read previews of the race and noted names like Ralph Hepburn, Cliff Bergere, Wilbur Shaw, Chet Miller and Rex Mays, his favorite.

Bugsy glanced at his shadow. It was nearing 11 a.m., the time the race would begin. There were acres to plant and seed to stir and no radio within a mile.

He returned to his papers. It was a day that belonged to cars and he scanned the ads. Studebaker offered a brand new Champion for sale at $695. Test pilot Andy McDonough, who had been at the controls when a Bell Aircobra P-39 plane made a dive at 600 miles per hour, recommended the Champion "for a thrilling performance."

DeSoto bragged about its simplimatic transmission, no shift getaway, no clutch operation. It carried an $898 price tag.

The Packard ads catered to a wealthier clientele. Its Clipper with electromatic drive started at $907 for two doors, $1,375 for four-door sedans.

Ford and Mercury didn't boast about their low prices. Just "get the facts and get a Ford." Mercury promised "big-car luxury with amazing thrift."

Bugsy and his dad stopped for lunch, sandwiches warmed by the sun.

"Sure wish I knew how Rex Mays was doing," Bugsy said. His dad offered encouragement. "He'll do okay. Always has."

Bugsy returned to his papers, convinced he'd have to wait until supper to learn who won the race. That changed a few minutes later when his big brother, who lived in Bedford, drove up in his '37 Ford. It was a holiday and he had the day off. The radio was on, voices shouting over the roar of engines.

Bugsy yelled, "It's a holiday for me, too, now that I can listen to the race."

Rex Mays was in contention. So was Wilbur Shaw until he crashed on Lap 151. Mauri Rose who had relieved Floyd Davis on about the 70th lap was moving up fast.

Bugsy, caught up in the drama, stirred the inoculent onto the beans at faster speeds. His dad finished the field before the race ended. He joined them near the radio.

Rose, driving the Noc-Out Hose Clamp, finished ahead of Mays in his Bowes Seal Fast car.

"Maybe Mays will win next year," Bugsy said.

His brother folded the papers for Bugsy, spied a theater ad, and said, "Cheer up little brother. We're going to see James Cagney and Pat O'Brien join the Air Marines in 'Devil Dogs of the Air' tonight."

* * *

Bugsy didn't know it at the time, but America would enter World War II before the year ended and the next 500-Mile Race would not be run until 1946.

Animal Lovers

Gordy was a dog's best friend, but even his buddies were surprised with his love for a mongrel that freezing January night in the 1940s.

They had just arrived back at Heltonville after a basketball game when Gordy spotted the shivering pup with mixed ancestry huddled on a step at the school.

He bent down, held out his hand and whispered, "Come here, boy." The stray eyed him cautiously, then walked slowly toward him, its tail too cold to waggle.

Gordy petted the pooch, gained its confidence, then raised it into his arms. "Hold the door for me," he said to Bogey.

The door he nodded toward led into the school boiler room where the big coal-fired furnace heated the steam which warmed the radiators in the classrooms. It had been left unlocked by the janitor who was at the restaurant on his break.

Inside, Gordy laid the dog gently on the concrete floor, close enough to feel the heat from the furnace. "He'll be warm here," Gordy said, smoothing the dog's matted coat.

Bogey said, "You're dreamin'. Bob will toss him outta here as soon as he gets back." Bob was the janitor.

Gordy shook his head. "Oh, no, he won't. He wouldn't dare after the story he told me the other day."

"What story?" the others seemed to ask in unison.

It was sometimes difficult to tell when Gordy was serious, being a teller of tall stories. He repeated the yarn Bob had told him about an incident at Stinesville, a town northwest of Bloomington which was about the size of Heltonville:

"A basketball player," he said, "had ridden into Stinesville on a horse for a Friday game. It was a cold night, like tonight, so the player decided to stay in town with a friend.

"The horse was accustomed to a stall in a warm barn on zero nights and his rider, being a kindly sort, didn't want to leave it outside. So he and his friend led it into the gym and around the sidelines, then down three or four steps to the boiler room. They tied it up and let it stay there all night."

Bogey wondered if the horse was all right the next morning.

Gordy grinned, "Yeah! Except for the mess behind him."

Someone said, "I'll bet the janitor was as mad as March."

Gordy laughed. "That's the good part. The janitor was the father of the friend, who helped the owner take the horse into the school. He—the janitor that is—cleaned up the poop piles and lead the horse outside the next morning before the teachers and students arrived.

"He never mentioned to the principal that the school had become a horse barn. It wouldn't be right to report his own son, or his house guest, to the principal, I guess."

Gordy's friends shook their heads in disbelief. "Good story, but we don't believe it," Bogey said.

They still thought it had been made up when Bob, the janitor, repeated the incident as he cleaned up after the stray pup the next morning.

"Some dog," he said affectionately, carrying it outside.

"Some story," Bogey said, unconvinced.

* * *

It was not until 1995, at a chance meeting of some men who had grown up at Stinesville, that the story finally was confirmed. One of the men, who had been a student at the time, was the son of the Stinesville janitor. It was sufficient evidence to erase 50 years of doubt by Gordy's friends.

A Starring Role

"Fatso" outgrew the word, but not the name.

Oh, he was overweight in elementary school, a bit hefty in junior high. But that was before he slimmed down as a teen-ager in the mid-1940s. By then, his weight was normal for a 5 feet 10 frame.

He was on the varsity basketball team at Heltonville, but, he was still "Fatso" to teammate and foe. His muscles bulged, evidence that he had done a man's job in the fields of summer, but farmers still called him "Fatso."

He didn't seem to mind. Outwardly, at least. The name didn't wipe the smile off his face or the humor from his tongue. He was quick-witted, a comic, a cut-up, who never seemed to have a down day.

Some teachers, who called him Lionel, thought "Fatso" was mischievous, a trouble-maker, a disruptive influence. He may have been. He was a product of his creativity, of a sharp mind he preferred to use for merriment, not maliciousness.

"Too bad, Lionel, doesn't use his brain in class as well as he does in the halls," more than one teacher said to another.

"Fatso" must have been a junior when he found an outlet for his talent. He learned the lines, studied the character, and was chosen for the lead in a school play.

His friends tormented him. "Imagine 'Fatso' on a theater marquee. 'Fatso Gable,' " they taunted. He answered each comment with a quick retort. He was serious at rehearsals, followed the script and performed the role perfectly. Teachers, who had been his classroom critics, agreed he had performed well. So did parents, who waited to congratulate him after the show.

He was in the limelight, the talk of the town for a few days.

Success didn't spoil "Fatso." It made him better. His conduct in class improved. So did his grades. Teachers remarked about the new Lionel. He still laughed and joked at recesses, even perpetrated a prank now and then. And despite the status to which he had been elevated, he didn't ask that "Fatso" be cast in a wastebasket of the past.

"Fatso" graduated, stayed around Heltonville for a while, then told friends he was headed "out west." Some guessed "out west" might be Hollywood, even though "Fatso" never gave a final destination.

He left town alone in search of his future. No one heard from him for years, not by phone, not by letter, not from a police agency or a hospital.

Some people thought he might have been a victim of foul play, his body gone, never to be found.

His friends preferred to think he was somewhere, alive and well, a success in a place where no one calls him "Fatso."

* * *

Postscript: About 40 years passed before his friends learned he was alive and well in another state where he had finally outgrown the "Fatso" label.

PART III

Special Places

Circumstances caused the "Country Bumpkin Gang," for the most part, to stay close to home. World War II and its gas and tire rationing, restricted travel. The government reminded motorists to ask themselves before leaving home, "Is this trip really necessary?"

Restrictions, though, did not limit a boy's imagination. Thoughts of the mind, generated by a curiosity whetted by literature and news reports, allowed him to escape his limited world with day dreams of remote places.

In their real world, a long-distant trip was rare. On a few occasions, some members of the gang, did travel out of state, returning with stories about the places they had visited.

Usually, however, trips were rides with truckers to the livestock market in Indianapolis or to the grain elevator at Medora. Sometimes, boys might visit the Jackson County Fair. Some accompanied their dads to Bedford, enjoying the experience, learning from strangers at the county courthouse and other places that offered new experience.

The "gang" swam nude in Back Creek, from April to September, bare roots of sycamore trees their diving boards. They would have been uncomfortable among city kids at the pool in Bedford and besides they had no swim suits to wear.

They fished at times, mostly to kill time, their thoughts adrift with the worms on the hooks that never seemed to attract the sun fish that reflected the sun that peaked through the limbs above.

When snow fell, they converted sheets of galvanized tin to sleds and raced down hills and across frozen streams, exhilarated by the speed, oblivious to the danger. And later, once they grew tired of outdoor excitement, they walked to their grandmothers' homes, knowing desserts awaited them.

On summer weekends, the boys biked to Norman for the free movies on Saturday nights. In the winter, they sought rides to Bedford to see double feature cowboy shows, moving on to the pool room as they grew older.

Barber shops were places to listen as men talked about politics or sports and argued more to entertain than convince.

Worship services were a must on Sunday, their parents told them, lest they void salvation. It was at those churches that they attended basket dinners, ice cream socials and other events.

There were special places, too, places like barn lofts converted to gymnasiums, streams and hollows where animal traps could be set, remote areas where they could savor silence, reflect on the changing seasons, appreciate nature that unfolded before them.

At home, on warm evenings, there was the front porch swing, a place that was special for the occupant of the moment.

It was the "Country Bumpkin Gang's" good fortune to enjoy life where they found it, to appreciate the environment in which they grew up, to play the hands they had been dealt. And they were better for it.

Generation Gap

It was a summer that had been so dull the mosquitoes were dying of boredom. Which explains why 10 to 12-year-old boys were eager for the annual event at the rural church they attended southeast of Heltonville.

"Basket dinner," they called it. To some adults it was an "all-day meeting," to others it was "homecoming."

Chig, Kin and their friends were more interested in what was in the baskets than what was in the sermons, which made the morning Sunday School and worship services which followed seem to last forever.

That changed, quickly and unexpectedly, however, when the preacher finished his sermon. "We can eat at last," Chig thought to himself. He was wrong. The Sunday School superintendent arose, adjusted the tie around his wilted shirt collar and announced it was time for the congregation to vote on whether to retain the minister for another year.

Anyone could vote, he said, which meant Chig, Kin and other youngsters who lined a back row were eligible to cast ballots, their vote a "yes" or a "no" on the blank pieces of paper they were given.

It was obvious the church elders weren't aware of the double wide generation gap between the pastor and the pre-teens. The preacher was, the boys thought, old, maybe even beyond 50, a man so conservative he dressed in dark suits and wore both suspenders and belt. And his sermons were long, at least to youngsters who counted time by the second rather than by the hour.

A new minister, they thought, might be short-winded and more attuned to their interests.

Chig was abrupt, insensitive, which explains why he wasn't content with a simple "yes" or a "no." "No! No! A Thousand Times No!" he scribbled on his ballot. He thought no more about his decision once the votes were collected.

Church was dismissed and he gathered with his friends under a shade tree until the women of the church had spread the food on the tables in the basement.

It was a smorgasbord no restaurant could match, selections unequalled, not even by the wives who served dinner for the threshing ring. Men and boys could gorge themselves, knowing they would be idle until milking and feeding time four hours away.

Chig ate quickly, heartily, then walked toward his dad who was in conversation with two other men and the preacher. His dad put his arm on Chig's shoulder and said, "You'll be happy to know, son, that the preacher here will be back for another year."

Chig hoped his sun-bronzed skin would hide the redness he felt spreading across his face.

"It was almost a unanimous vote, except for a few 'noes' that looked like they were written by some boys," his dad added. Chig knew the concrete on the floor was too thick to open and swallow him. He stood frozen in the sweltering, cramped basement when the preacher said:

"If you know who wrote 'No! No! A Thousand Times No,' I'd like to talk to that boy to see if maybe we could come to some kind of understanding. I sure don't want any unhappy church members, especially young folks."

Kin became Chig's friend for life at that instant. "Come on Chig," he yelled from the steps to the outside door.

"See you later," Chig told the men, thankful for avoiding a reply to the preacher. His hurried steps gave no trace of the load of food he carried inside him. The day had brought even more excitement than he had anticipated.

A "Boaring" Day

Buster lived in Bedford, hadn't been in the country often and thought nothing exciting ever happened "out in the sticks."

He called places outside the city limits "the sticks." That's why he happened to be in Heltonville that Saturday in the 1940s. On a dare.

Tyke had challenged him to spend the day. "I guarantee you some surprises before the day is over," he'd said.

Buster agreed. "If there is not surprise, you owe me a dollar. If so, I owe you one."

Buster wasn't easily impressed. He complained, "You call this excitement?" as they sat in the barber shop watching matted hair tumble to the floor.

He complained about the dust at the feed mill where they watched wheat being ground into flour.

They'd played a few games of rotation at Pete's Pool Room, even sneaked into a back room and fed a few nickels and dimes to the slot machines Pete kept out of sight of the law. Buster admitted he hadn't seen one-armed bandits before, let alone play them, but added, "I'm still not surprised or excited."

"This could be a long day," Tyke thought to himself. They went to the school playground, shot a few baskets at the outside goal, but Buster whined, "We could play indoors at Bedford."

"Ever been to a general store?" Tyke asked.

Buster said he didn't think so. He followed Tyke through the Roberts general store, past the grocery, into the hardware section and out into the feed building. Buster wasn't awe struck. "I think you've lost a dollar," he told Tyke, who replied that the day wasn't over.

A smile arched across Tyke's mouth as he saw Fred park his pickup in front of the store. "I think my day is about to get brighter," he said, leaving Buster mystified, curious.

Fred walked behind the pickup, opened the tailgate, called out a name and watched as his big 400-pound Chester White boar leaped to the ground.

The boar followed Fred to the door, waddled into the store and trailed his master around the stove, snorting what seemed like greetings to loafers in the liar's chairs. Fred talked for a while as the boar stood still, his conduct exemplary as he eyed the crowd. He followed when Fred called his name, walked out the door to the back of the truck, waited for a ramp to be in place and scampered back into the pickup.

Buster appeared stunned. "Come on," Tyke said, "let's run down to the barber shop and watch."

Fred stopped at the barber shop, again opened the tailgate, led the boar inside and let it stand in the back while he joined the conversation. Buster was still silent, staring in amazement at Fred's pet. It was a scene he wouldn't see in Bedford.

Again Fred called the boar's name and it followed as he walked from the shop, then took its place in the pickup bed. Buster followed Tyke from the shop, pulled out a thin billfold and removed a dollar.

"If this happens every Saturday, I'll be back next week with some friends from town," he said, adding, "Maybe I can win a dollar from each of them."

Tyke laughed. "Can't guarantee it, but if Fred knows there are some visitors in town, he'll want to show them life ain't all dull out here in the sticks."

Sparring Partners

May had arrived and with it the Saturday night fight at Norman.

It was the early 1940s, back when C. E. Cummings auctioned off furniture and other items from a platform beside his store before treating folks to a free movie on the side of the building across the street. It was the auction, and the movies, adults came to see.

Boys who were too young to be attracted to girls came to see the weekly fight. The card was always the same: Floggin' Froggie vs. Whalin' Walt.

Froggie and Walt were in their teens; as opposite as A and Z, as unlikely to mix as water and oil. They didn't care much for each other, for reasons fight fans never learned. Maybe it was because their interests were as different as their backgrounds.

Froggie was maybe 5 feet 9, stocky, a bit muscular, the son of a day laborer who worked for farmers between Heltonville and Norman. He had almost enough brothers and sisters to cover a baseball field.

He lived in a small frame home on a few acres off Ind. 58. Froggie talked a lot, usually in wise cracks, laughed often and saw humor where others might see darkness. He could roll a cigarette from a pack of Bull Durham and light a match with a swish across the seat of his overalls.

Everybody liked Froggie, except Walt, and that was probably Froggie's own fault. Walt was one of three children of a more prosperous farmer who lived at the edge of Norman. Walt was tall, maybe 6 feet 2, willowy, more interested in books and school than in small talk. He didn't smoke, didn't talk much.

His only known enemy was Froggie, and that may have been his own fault for not being more open to banter, more vocal, more given to back talk which Froggie seemed to enjoy.

Whatever! It was a personality conflict which could be counted on to erupt into a fight if the two were together more than 20 seconds.

A word, or a look, could launch all out war. The encounters weren't sissy-like shoving matches. They were down and dirty, no holds barred, no conditional surrender, fights.

No one had to egg on either Walt or Froggie. Young observers like Tyke, Tad, Bugsy and other pre-teens watched, partial to neither, forming a barrier, lest the combatants rolled onto Ind. 58 as they tumbled onto the ground, bound by wrestling holds.

Froggie usually won, being less inhibited, more of a street fighter. That changed one night. He had Walt on the ground, a fist drawn for a punch to the head.

Walt realized his peril, reached out with his right hand, found a small geode in the gravel and crashed it under Froggie's nose.

Froggie spat out chips of two teeth between bloody lips. He released his hold and grabbed his mouth. The fight was over for the night.

Walt showed up the next Saturday night with two pair of boxing gloves. "Mom made them," he said.

She couldn't prevent the fight, but she could make it less likely the brawlers would be hurt. Observers laughed. Froggie didn't. He raked his tongue against his broken teeth and accepted the wisdom of boxing gloves.

The fights grew less vicious as Walt and Froggie grew older and argued instead of pummeling each other.

Truth is the conflicts became so mild, teenagers passed them up for the free shows. Froggie and Walt grew from youths to men, went their separate ways.

Froggie never forgot the fights, his front teeth wouldn't let him. Chances are Walt remembered, too, each time he picked up a geode or thought about those home-made boxing gloves.

An Open Top

It was quiet time in Norman that Saturday night in the early 1940s. Adults were seated on cross ties watching the weekly free movie C. E. Cummings showed on the side of his store. Teen-age girls who teen-age boys had come to town to impress were seated near their protective parents, the time for conversation past.

The movies didn't interest John, Gene and Tad. They were too adventurous to sit through an old film which had to be spliced three or four times per reel. They relished something, anything, that offered more excitement.

That something came when John noticed his brother leave with a friend. "Hey, Dan's gone, but his Model A is still here. Let's go for a ride," he suggested.

John was six weeks past his 15th birthday, too young to have a driver's license. No matter. Like most farm teens, he knew how to drive, be it a tractor, truck or car. And, he knew there would be no sheriff's deputies within miles of town.

Tad and Gene, who also were 15, squeezed into the coupe beside him, expecting a leisurely ride.

John, however, drove south out of Norman like he was attempting to qualify for a jalopy race. He made it around two sharp turns, the back tires shooting gravel through the fences at each, then accelerated as he headed down a decline.

The warm August air felt cool as it entered the rolled down windows. "Wonder how fast I can make this turn?" John asked, not giving his passengers time to answer as he roared into a 90-degree turn to the west onto another gravel road. He would never know the answer to his question.

The Model A skidded on the loose gravel, flipped on its left side, propelling John, Tad and Gene through the top, which was a combination of wooden slats, heavy cloth and tar. They landed in a stack, John at the bottom, Gene in the middle and Tad on top.

The Ford coughed and died. Tad stood up, coughed himself, spit dirt and reached for John with one hand while brushing off his clothes with the other. John remained on the ground, his hands, bloodied by stones, feeling his legs to make sure no bones were broken. He eased himself to his feet, took two steps and decided he'd survive.

Together, they flipped the car back onto its wheels. Tad and Gene waited to see if it would start before climbing in, reluctantly, next to a now sullen driver.

John drove back to town as slowly as a farmer on his way to pick up his wife from a quilting party. His voice was soft as it had been loud. He was more concerned about the condition of the car than with speed.

"Dan will kill me," he said. "I don't have enough money to have it fixed, Dan doesn't have enough to pay for it himself, either."

Gene allowed as how he might be able to scrape up a few dollars. Tad visualized the money he'd made baling hay being withdrawn from a savings account once Dan demanded payment.

At Norman, John parked the car in the same spot he'd found it. He was still sitting on the running board when Tad left for home with a farewell: "See you next week, unless Dan comes after me before that."

Tad was apprehensive the next few days. He expected Dan was coming for money each time a cloud of dust rose along the county road. Dan never showed up.

Tad didn't see him until that Saturday night in Norman. A girl was seated beside him in the Model A, its torn, battered top removed. The roofed coupe had become an open top, a convertible of sorts. Dan had turned a disaster into an asset that made him an object of envy.

Tad's earnings were safe. So was the money John and Gene had worried about raising.

Dan stopped the car next to Tad. "The next time you take a joy ride with John, you won't have to worry about going through the roof." He grinned as he checked his hair in the rear view mirror that remained on the windshield that had survived the crash.

Swing Time

Porch swings were for dreamers and thinkers, for endless recollection and boundless imagination.

Oh, anyone could still sit in them. But they didn't mean as much to those who just sat and swayed, letting the swing work more than their minds.

Swings moved easily on creaking chains attached to the ceiling of porches that stretched along the front of farm houses. They were made of wooden slats, painted and repainted and painted again, some etched with initials carved by youngsters with new pocket knives.

Swings at farm homes east of Heltonville on summer days were reserved for no one. They belonged to the occupants of the moment, who were not dislodged easily. And they were seldom vacant, especially in the evenings.

Those were the best times for the dreamers and thinkers. Boys like Chig and Tyke and Bugsy could relax after a day in the fields, the milking done, the cream separated from the milk. They could let their thoughts run free as the rabbits which bounded from wheat shocks at threshing time.

They might look forward to the July Fourth holiday ahead, think about new bikes they were saving for, dream of game-saving catches or game-winning hits on the baseball diamond, of winning shots in basketball games, of service as Royal Canadian mounties.

They could travel as far as their creative fuel would take them, do what they would not dare in real life, escape to other continents and travel to far-away planets. They could be whatever they wanted to be.

Like most youngsters, though, they seldom stayed put in one place. They'd vacate the swings, sometimes holding them for their grandparents to back onto.

Grandparents didn't talk much. They just sat together, holding hands, maybe thinking back over the years, recalling their lives together, the kids they had raised, the grandchildren they had coddled. Sometimes they'd smile for no reason, except that they were still together. They left the swing at dusk. It was their bed time, even though the chickens were still up and the birds were still chirping.

Mothers and fathers took over the swing. They had more worries. Would the rain come in time to save the crops? Would there be money to pay the real estate taxes? Would there be enough egg and cream money to send the kids to the Jackson County fair as well as the Independence Day celebration?

Yet, it was quiet time for them, a time to reflect on the day that was about to end, to look ahead to tomorrow and work to be done. They didn't stay late for morning on farms came early.

A daughter's boy friend had arrived and the swing would be their rendezvous until 11, 11:30 or until a parent's order from an upstairs bedroom sent the young man shuffling off in the darkness.

Occasionally, on a hot night, a youngster unafraid of the dark might escape the oppression of the humidity from a tin roof to find relief on the swing, his feet sticking out over the rail. He'd still be there at daybreak to be awakened by his mother or his dad, too agile to moan about an aching back or tired bones.

The swings were havens, too, on Sunday afternoons. A place for the preacher who had come to dinner to sit with his wife and doze off after a dinner of chicken and dumplings, roast beef, cake and apple pie.

Adults sat in uncomfortable porch chairs and watched, knowing he'd be gone in time for them to have a few minutes aboard later.

* * *

A day seldom passed when the swing wasn't used. It would hang there until fall came, its season of purpose served. It then would be pulled against the ceiling, there to remain until spring.

Saturday Date

Eddie drove his car into a ford in Back Creek and started lathering it with suds from a brick of lye soap.

Tad, Tyke and Bugsy were downstream, swimming nude, when they noticed the white caps drift into their deep pocket of water.

Tyke said, "I'm gettin' outta here. If I wanted to take a bath in soap, I'd go home and jump in the wash tub." It was an April Saturday in the early 1940s and the only running water in most rural homes east of Heltonville came from a stream or a spring.

Tad and Bugsy followed Tyke, letting the sun be their towel, before pulling on their pants and shirts.

School had been in summer recess less than 10 days, but they were barefoot, the soles of their feet already as tough as harness leather.

They rode their bikes a few hundred yards along the creek bank, pulled onto a dirt lane and spotted Eddie's car. Eddie was about 18, five, six years older than they, but he was their neighbor, friend and liaison between adolescence and adulthood.

The car was his prized possession and he had saved what he earned working for farmers, talked his mom out of some cream and egg money and borrowed the rest of the cost from his dad.

It was a 1937 Ford V-8 with narrow running boards and chrome from front to back. A spinner knob was on the steering wheel which was covered with cloth to imitate a zebra's skin. A squirrel's tail dangled from the radio antenna. Mud flaps, with reflectors, hung from the front fenders.

Eddie washed the soap from the car, toweled it dry and used a chamois to bring out the shine. The black paint glistened in the sun that penetrated the still-nude sycamore branches. He shook a can of cleaner and scrubbed the tar and dirt from the three-inch-wide white walls on the four tires.

Tyke, Tad and Bugsy cleaned the chrome until they could see the contortions of their shadows.

"Thanks," Eddie said, pulling a cheap pocket watch from the bib of his overalls. "Gotta get a hair cut, take a bath, get cleaned up and pick up this girl for a night on the town."

He stopped without explanation, opened the car door, removed the ash tray and emptied the butts on the creek bank. "Sure wouldn't want my date tonight to see someone else's lipstick on those cigarettes," he said.

"Do we know her?" Bugsy asked.

"Doubt it," Eddie said, "she's from Bedford. But keep it quiet. I still wanta keep some girls from around here on the string." His young friends nodded. It was a tacit agreement that needed no confirmation.

Eddie drove off slowly, careful not to stir up dust that would ruin the wash.

The next morning Eddie drove into the church parking lot, the whitewalls on his V-8 red with mud, the fenders smeared from an overnight rain.

"Don't look so sad," he told his young friends. "It didn't rain until after I took her home from the midnight show. She said my V-8 was the prettiest car she'd ever been in."

"What did she think about you?" Tyke asked.

Eddie winked, like he'd keep that a secret. "If you'd agree to wash my car, I wouldn't even tell you."

A few weeks later Eddie stored his V-8 in the shed on the barn. Uncle Sam had called him to duty with the U.S. Army.

Echoes Of The Past

Leaves pave Henderson Creek road as they do each autumn, creating a nature trail in the past.

It is a trail that winds back 50 years or so, back to a time when the books closed on the Works Progress Administration and Civilian Conservation Corps, the last chapters of the Great Depression written.

World War II was underway, ending make-work projects that widened roads, deepened side ditches, built parks, developed recreation sites. Infrastructure was not yet a highfalutin word, but government-employed men, working for $2 a day, improved what there was, then added to it.

Here in Henderson Creek valley just west of Norman, a few miles northeast of Heltonville, was an example of what government make-work had accomplished. Folks who lived nearby called it "Hecky Martin's dam site" or just "Hecky Martin's." Hecky's name became a part of geography, a place rather than an individual.

Hecky owned the land where the WPA and CCC workers built the dam, shaped a beach below it, created picnic grounds, making a retreat for individuals and families to relax from the rigors of the farm, the stone mills and the logging woods.

It was, as all things are when new, busy, appreciated, manicured, cleaned after use. In summer months, bathers lined the beach. The more daring swam in the deeper pool above the dam.

Students from Heltonville and Clearspring met on cool October evenings at Hecky's dam for picnics and class parties. Individuals congregated for unsupervised pleasure.

There was no vandalism. Not at first. It was a recreational oasis in a parkless desert. And it was proof that government could be a servant of the people, that its resources could be used to benefit the poor as well as the wealthy.

It wasn't noticeable at first, but the newness gradually wore off, the grounds given less care. It remained, though, a place for fun and pleasure. That changed after Leonis East, who lived a few miles away, drowned one night in the water above the dam.

Men called it "a bad job," their words for a tragedy. Their sons, not yet teens, had trouble comprehending the finality of it.

Visitors continued to use the park for a while; continued to care for the grounds for a time. Attendance gradually declined. The war did that. Most men 17 and older traded swim trunks for sailors' and soldiers' uniforms. Young women had gone to work in defense plants. No one seemed to care about the place.

Maybe it was because there was no one to supervise the teens who remained, teens trapped in an uncertain future, unsure of what the world held in store.

In the end it was the area's young, boys too young to fight, maybe even some girls, who destroyed what had been built primarily as a place for them to enjoy.

Restrooms were damaged, buildings marred, grounds littered. And there was no one in those years of war to rebuild what they had ruined. In a few years there was no "Hecky Martin's," no dam, no beach, no picnic grounds, no class parties, no sounds of laughter.

Today there are only echoes of the past and an overgrown lane, barely detectable from Henderson Creek Road, the only clue of what once was.

And memories covered with autumn leaves.

Tin Town

If Tad had a choice, he preferred only his father's company on trips to Bedford.

Oh, he enjoyed his mother's company, too. But she didn't like to stop at some of the places his father did. Places like Al's sandwich shop, the courthouse and Tin Town.

Tad knew he would get a good fish sandwich at Al's. He would enjoy the banter among men at the courthouse. And a stop at the little store along the railroad spur in Tin Town would certainly remind his dad of a story.

Tin Town was an area along Ind. 58, also known as Heltonville Road, in northeast Bedford. It was the nearest thing, around 1940, that Bedford had to a slum.

Tad never learned the real name of the operator of the Tin Town store. His dad, like all the other customers, called him Poopie for a reason they didn't explain.

It wasn't the best store in town, wasn't even as big as the general stores in Heltonville and Norman. It was convenient, though, being on the way home.

Tad's dad always found a reason to stop. "The man needs the business," he explained. "And something interesting is always happening around Tin Town."

Men, who lived nearby, huddled around the coal stove, getting warmer there than they could at their homes, which had no insulation. They eyed strangers curiously unless Poopie called them by name, like he did Tad's father.

It was a man's world, and Tad noticed few women ever shopped at the store.

A "what's new?" would bring a verbal monologue from Poopie that, reduced to type, would fill two news columns in the Bedford Times.

Back in the car, Tad's father usually said, "Well, so much for Tin Town today."

Tad had wondered, on his first visit, why the area was called Tin Town.

"I imagine," his dad replied, "it was because at one time some of the homes were tin shacks. I remember back eight to ten years ago when a lot of the shacks and shanties burned. Some people said the fires were an improvement, but it wasn't their homes, such as they were, that burned.

Tad asked if Tin Town was a part of Bedford.

"It's in the city limits, but it's pretty much ignored other than that. At one time folks called Jim Elkins the mayor of Tin Town, but that was just to make him feel good."

He laughed, then recalled an incident back in the 1920s when police had to break up a free-for-all in Tin Town. "By the time the fracas was over, people forgot what started it," he said.

At home, Tad told his mom about their stop in Tin Town.

"I don't even like to drive by that place. And I certainly don't know why your dad likes to stop at the store," she sighed.

"I don't either. But I'm glad he does."

* * *

The area of Bedford gradually changed. Today there are no shacks in the area. And only men with long memories ever mention Tin Town.

Sugar And Spice

Mrs. J.'s grandsons were usually well behaved when they visited, knowing good conduct would be rewarded with chocolate cake and apple pie.

Late winter was a special time, though, a time when each acted even nicer than normal.

The five of them, Billy, Bob, Ray, Tad and Tyke, visited her almost every winter Saturday, aware that was the day she baked.

All lived within a mile of her farm home near Heltonville and the warm, fresh items from her oven tasted good after their short, but cold walks.

They tried to pay for the treats she served by splitting wood and filling the box near the stove or by carrying water from the spring. That effort never seemed equal to the hours she spent around the stove, and they always asked if there were other chores they could do.

She usually turned down those requests, knowing they had cows to milk and livestock to care for at their own homes.

"Are you sure there's nothing you need us to do?" Bob asked one Saturday in late February.

Mrs. J. wiped her hands in her apron. "Being as you are all here, and the maple sap will be running soon, you can get things ready down at the sugar house for Joe."

Joe was her son, who helped her make the syrup.

"The sugar house" was a small building, maybe 20 by 30 feet, that was over the hill down by the spring. It was there that the sap from the maples was brought and boiled into syrup.

Bob, the oldest, led the way, cleaning cloths in hand. He assigned Tad and Tyke to the buckets, Billy to the spiles, Ray to the wagon. "I'll clean the boiling pan and the rake," he said.

There were 100 or so buckets, unused since the previous March when they caught the sap that flowed through the spiles that Billy cleaned. Ray swept, then removed the dust from the 100-gallon tank that sat on the frame of a wagon with wide steel wheels that wouldn't mire in the mud of spring.

The boiling pan, about 6 feet wide, 12 feet long, 6 to 8 inches deep had been bottom up since the last syrup season ended. Bob asked for help in turning it upright.

He cleaned the wide, wooden rake which was pulled through the sap to keep it from burning as it was condensed to syrup.

"How much sap does it take to make a gallon?" Tad wondered.

Bob said, "About 75 when Grandma makes it. Some people can make a gallon with 50 gallons of sap, but it's not as good as grandma's."

Billy said, "Ain't nobody's syrup better than hers."

Tyke agreed, stepping outside to sweep the snow off the wood Joe had stacked nearby. Joe and Mrs. J. would know just how much wood, how much heat, to use to boil the sap.

The grandsons returned to the house after a couple of hours and reported what they had done.

Mrs. J. thanked them. "You've been especially helpful today," she said. "There's more pie and cake if that will take care of the bill."

Her grandsons looked at each other. The dessert was ample pay. Their bonus would come in a couple of weeks when she sent them home with gallon cans of new maple syrup and a reminder to return the next day for her annual stir-off.

A "stir-off" was a big family event. It was a day when her children, her grandchildren and some friends would stir bowls filled with maple syrup into hardened sugar candy, unequaled by Babe Ruth or Three Musketeer bars.

A boy would do a lot of chores—and behave for an entire year—for a treat like that.

PART IV

Lessons Of Life

School for the "Country Bumpkin Gang" mirrored life, sometimes good, sometimes bad, indifferent on occasions.

Rural students rode buses into Heltonville, watched the seasons unfold, gazed out from the windows as nature painted new murals from September to April. In the fall of the late 1930s, dust from the Great Plains browned the yellow hacks. In winters, snows clogged the narrow gravel roads; spring thaws and heavy rains made them quagmires.

A trustee administered the school, which had 300 or so students in 12 grades. Some teachers seemed old, having taught for 20 or more years; others were young, fresh out of college, young women from cities unaccustomed to the ways of the country.

Restrooms—green in color, fly-invested in September, freezing in January—were down cinder paths.

Most students brought their lunches, it being a time before cafeterias and vending machines. When old enough, the "Bumpkins" walked down the hill to the restaurant, adding ice cream cones to the peanut butter sandwiches they'd eaten on the way.

One day followed another, with little new, for the first six years the "Bumpkins" were in school. That changed suddenly and their lives would never be the same. They listened over the radio—in the assembly room at school—that Monday when Congress declared war. It was the day after the Japanese ravaged

Pearl Harbor and made December 7, 1941, a date that would live in infamy.

Most of the school, including the gym, burned the next April. Junior high classrooms, for the next two years, would be in the Christian Church basement. As freshmen, the "Bumpkins" moved up to the part of the school that was saved from the fire.

It would be years after they graduated before they realized that education comes from books, teachers and concentration, not from bricks, stone and mortar.

Summer's End

Tad had never noticed how much life changed each summer. But he had never been 12 before, never was as curious as he had become about the things around him.

It was the early 1940s, the year unimportant, for his experience was no different than that of dozens of other farm youths his age, whatever the time.

He was growing up, learning that nothing remained the same, that time stood still only on a stopped clock, that change was inevitable.

He looked down at his overall pant legs which were above his ankles. He had grown two inches since school at Heltonville ended back in April.

Now it was August and the fields and woodland that thrived in the spring languished under the unrelenting sun.

He whistled for Rover, then called him. Rover didn't come, preferring to do his panting in the shade on the east side of the big farm house. It was a dog day and Rover preferred it to be a one of rest.

No problem, Tad decided. He would walk to his private swimming hole down in the creek, enjoy the time alone. He waved to his mom who was in the garden, now mostly weeds, except for a few cucumbers and potatoes, both Irish and sweet, which could be dug in a week or two.

He noticed the grass in the yard was dormant, less green, than it had been earlier. Only the plantain and buck horn thrived.

He stepped out into the dirt driveway which had turned to dust, noticed a car on the gravel road stir a cloud of red which drifted out into the barn lot. The pasture was brown, its ground as hard as the soapstone in the creek bottoms.

Cows grazed where they could find green foliage, sometimes gnawing at ragweeds which ruined their milk and spoiled the butter. Steers had given up the search, taking cover in the shade. Calves born at winter's end, now emancipated from their mothers, explored the fence rows.

A spring colt had grown up, too, its friskiness in hiatus until the sun sank over the hill to the west.

Ground under trees was bare, what moisture there had been in the soil stolen by the roots of the beech, oak and poplar trees.

Tad walked by the hog lot. Pigs wallowed in what water was left in the pool they had rooted. Sows, he noticed, had sought fresh water and found it in a vein they had rooted open in the side of the hill.

The straw stack that had been bright, reflective in the sun 10 days earlier, already was showing dull brown. Corn stalks, dark green just a few weeks ago, were yellowing at the bottom, the silks dark, much of the pollen gone from the tassels.

Tad reached the swimming hole, stripped off his clothes and slid into the water, warm, no longer invigorating as it had been on those cool days of May. He cleared the pool of the thin bark the sycamore tree had dropped.

The water was stagnant, a stream no longer running from the creek into the pool. He climbed out, dried in the sun, turning slowly in a complete circle to review nature's newest picture. Spring paradise lost, he would, he decided, have to accept summer's end. He had learned that nothing lasts forever, that life, like the seasons, has its own cycles.

Sartorial Splendor

Stan, the barber, took the drape off the farmer in the chair, put the money he was paid in a drawer, and shouted, "Next!"

Bugsy closed the Captain Marvel comic book, laid it on the bench that once was a church pew, and lifted himself into the hydraulic chair. His summer of contentment was about to end.

In a few days he would give up the freedom of the farm for the confinement of the classroom. Textbooks, not comic books, would become his reading material. It had been a good vacation, that summer of 1941.

Bugsy had turned 12, drifting between boyhood and manhood, a child at times, a man on other occasions. He was old enough to work in the fields, young enough to swim nude in sycamore lined creeks.

Stan pinned the cover on Bugsy, who quickly ran his right index finger around his neck to loosen the restraint. The barber forced his fine-toothed comb through Bugsy's matted and tangled hair, then tried to find a part. "Haven't seen you for a while," Stan said.

"Nope. Ain't been in all summer," Bugsy replied.

Stan asked, "Want a regular cut?"

"Yep," Bugsy replied.

Stan laid the comb on the counter, picked up the clippers, paused and said, "When you go back to school Friday, you may want to say, 'Yes' and 'No' instead of 'yep' and 'nope' and stop using the word 'ain't.' "

Stan clipped, snipped and talked. Bugsy's hair tumbled in clumps onto the oiled tongue-and-groove wooden floor. Bugsy felt as naked as a sheared sheep. "That about does it," Stan said, proud of his work. He rubbed a few splashes of tonic from a long-neck bottle into Bugsy's hair, combed it, unfastened the cover, sprinkled some powder onto a brush and flipped off the loose hair.

"Want me to add some rose oil to make you smell good?" he asked.

Bugsy shrugged his shoulders. "Don't want to smell like a girl," he replied emphatically.

Stan spun the chair so Bugsy could see himself in the big mirror that lined the south wall. "Hope you don't mind being two-toned."

"Two-toned!" Bugsy muttered. "I look more like night and day." His face and lower neck, bronzed by months in the sun, accentuated the white ring around his head where the hair had been removed. He was even more self-conscious than most 12-year-olds about how he appeared to others.

"Much obliged," he said, paying Stan.

"You may want to say thank you' instead of 'much obliged' to your teachers," Stan said, offering more advice at no charge.

Bugsy nodded as he walked out the door, thinking he was being taught even before school started.

* * *

The U.S. would be at war in four months. The restraints of a barber's neck cover would seem trivial, a boy's red face, white head unimportant. Realities of war would replace comic book fiction. The age of innocence would end. No summer would ever be the same.

School Daze

Mothers shopped, fathers winced, dollar signs danced in the eyes of merchants.

The back-to-school brigade enjoyed the attention.

City folks stayed home. The time was any Saturday before Labor Day, any year from 1935 to 1945. The place was Courthouse Square in Bedford. Rural schools like Heltonville had opened the previous day, but only long enough for teachers to meet their students, issue book lists for classes which would start the following Tuesday.

It was now parents turn to buy those books, yellow Golden Rod notebooks, crayons, rulers, paste and scissors. And to select durable clothes which would last for eight months despite 35 or so scrubbings with lye soap on washboards.

Every parking spot on the square was taken. So were those on streets for blocks in each direction. Banks were busy. Some farmers cashed checks for grain and livestock sales; others negotiated loans.

Wives waited for the extra cash to add to the crinkled bills they had taken from cookie jars, for they would need all the money they could raise to buy what their youngsters needed.

Textbooks came before clothes. Old clothes could be patched if necessary; books had to be new for there were no rentals, no free texts. Parents crowded into the only book store in town, elbowing their way toward harried clerks who filled orders quickly.

Fathers carried the books to the car.

Mothers took their sons to Keller's if they could afford Oshkosh B'Gosh overalls, to Penney's for Big Macs, if not. They also bought durable shoes that could be worn in the barn lot as well as in school, denim shirts, underwear, long johns and briefs, socks, sock caps and warm coats.

Girls were harder to please, spent more time selecting clothes and patterns from which their moms could make dresses.

Some fathers, their wallets as thin as their patience, escorted their sons to the barber shop to be "sheared," as they called it. Others, knowing their summer of companionship was about to end, took their boys to cafes for fish sandwiches and conversation.

Most of the men congregated later around the courthouse, recalling for their sons the one-room schools they attended, the slates, instead of notebooks and chalkboards, they used, the teachers they had tormented.

By mid-afternoon, the men began to tug pocket watches from the bib of their overalls to check the time. Milking time was drawing near. They'd check the car, mutter a few barnyard words when their wives and daughters had not returned, swore some more and waited.

On the way home, parents reviewed their expenditures for the day, assessed their bank balances. None ever complained about the high cost of parenthood.

Their children paid little attention. They were too busy checking out their new clothes. And at looking at literature books that would widen their imagination and geography texts that would take them far beyond the Lawrence County square in Bedford.

Brains Over Brawn

Bub had finished his freshman year back in April, 5 feet 4, 110 pounds of doubt in search of himself. He had spent that spring in the early 1940s with his eyes on an eighth grade beauty instead of on his textbooks.

Once in a while she'd smile and return his look, but otherwise paid little attention to him. It seemed to Bub that she preferred men who were older, wiser, taller and stronger.

It was about that time that Bub picked up a Superman comic book at the barber shop in Heltonville. The same ad was on the back cover as it always was; a picture of Charles Atlas and an illustration of a once 90-pound, skinny weakling being kicked with sand at the beach.

Bub identified with the one-time weakling. It could have been him, except the nearest beach was 30 miles away at Spring Mill State Park. If he had any money, he would have ripped the page from the book, taken it home, filled out the coupon for the body building course and mailed it.

He knew his parents couldn't afford the cost, even if he told them he could become a Charles Atlas, strong enough to support the world on his shoulders.

It didn't help his confidence when the barber said, "See you later, Peanut."

"Peanut!" "Peadad!" "Shrimp!" Bub had heard the taunts, had been told he was "no bigger than a pound of soap." Now, he convinced himself, he would do something about it. He could do nothing about his height, but he could build up his body, putting muscles on his arms, expanding his chest, tightening his legs.

It would take discipline, he knew. He would, he told himself, spend the summer working in hayfields, chopping weeds from corn, picking tomatoes, doing whatever work he could find on farms around town.

He soon became a favorite of farmers, a boy doing a man's work. They told each other about him, this wisp of a lad with a big heart.

Almost each night, no matter how tired, Bub lifted weights in the garage, adding a heavier load each day. Each time he thought of giving up, the object of his affection, the target of his dream, danced across his thoughts. Slowly his arms thickened, his legs tightening like posts.

Nature was changing Bub, too. His legs grew out from his pant legs. He didn't notice the change at first, never bothered to measure his height, until his mom mentioned it. He was in metamorphosis, changing from a boy to a man.

By late August, he was 5 feet 7 inches, 140 pounds of muscle, vigor and vitality. He had made himself into a miniature Charles Atlas.

He could not wait until school started anew. Except when he waved as she drove through town with her parents, he had not seen the girl since school was out.

He marched to school early that first September day, waiting for the buses to arrive, eager for her to see the new Bub. He planted a smile across his face, ready to greet her as she walked toward the building.

The smile collapsed when he saw her, hand in hand with a newcomer Bub did not recognize. She smiled at Bub, but continued to listen as the new kid talked. He was shorter than she, wore thick glasses, was thin as a rail, stooped slightly at the shoulders and was more bone than muscle.

It seemed obvious, he had never seen a Charles Atlas ad. The girl, Bub concluded, preferred brains to brawn. Bub slumped against the bricks. His summer's work had been wasted, he thought.

He would never look at another girl, he told himself. He was heartbroken. He stayed that way for 10 minutes . . . until one of the sophomore girls noticed he had become someone worth their attention.

The Box Social

Bogey was at that age in life when he thought the sun rose to hear him crow. He talked a lot, mostly about himself.

Life was a stage and he was its main player. Or so he imagined. He kept his hair plastered with Brilliantine and combed it between classes and at recess, usually when he imagined the eyes of all the junior high girls were watching. He was impressed with his own image.

If there was no mirror around, he'd preen until he saw himself in a window glass. His reflection always awarded him with a look of approval.

It was no wonder he looked forward to the seventh grade box social. Each of the girls, he imagined, would want him to bid on the treats they brought.

He was rich only in self-importance. He had no more money to spend than any of the other boys in his class.

That's why it was easy for Bugsy and Tad to rig the bidding when time came to auction off the box dinners. An explanation later. First some background.

Box socials were fund-raising events. Girls brought fancy decorated boxes usually wrapped in colorful crepe paper. But they carried them in plain brown paper sacks to keep the boys from knowing who had brought what box, which would have spoiled the mystery of the auction.

Each box was to be sold to the highest bidder, the price rising a penny or a nickel a bid. The auction was as suspenseful as a blind date, the winning bidder not knowing which girl he would dine with until she was identified.

Tad and Bugsy knew Bogey had his eye on one of the prettiest girls in class. "We know which box she brought," Bugsy told him, pointing out one with white paper and a red ribbon.

"How much money do you have?" Tad asked.

Bogey brought two quarters from his pocket.

Bugsy told him to start the bidding at a dime. "Tad and I will bid it up to make this look legit, then let you buy it for less than 50 cents."

The plot sounded good to Bogey. He shouted out his bids and looked as proud as a peacock when the teacher-auctioneer said, "Sold to Bogey for 45 cents."

Bogey waited for the pretty girl to step forward, thank him for buying her lunch and waltz him off to seats in the corner. Instead, a girl who was a mile from pretty and a foot from thin, grabbed him by the arm. She looked as pleased as Bogey appeared stunned for being victimized by Tad and Bugsy.

The crowd applauded for the girl was smart, pleasant and well-liked.

Tad and Bugsy tried not to look at the couple as they dined, but a red glow from Bogey's face made him difficult to ignore.

By chance, Bugsy's bid won him dinner with the girl Bogey had hoped to impress.

Bogey didn't speak to either Bugsy or Tad for a couple of days. He was back to his old important self by then. "Thanks for fixing me up the other night. I'll be getting better grades this semester since I have the smartest girl in class to help me."

He wasn't about to admit he had been bested in a contest of prankmanship.

Strong Soap

It was a mild expletive, innocuous by standards of the 1990s, that earned Pokey a rebuke that March morning 50 years ago.

He had used the word to describe the weather. The teacher would have preferred he use other terms. She suggested "wet, damp, foggy, even miserable" instead.

Pokey, though, was in an argumentative mood. He repeated his description, which upset the teacher even more. "I'd advise your mother to buy a bar of soap to wash out your mouth when you talk like that," she said, unable to hide her anger.

She looked even more disturbed when Pokey explained, "My mom doesn't buy bars of soap." Pokey always looked scrubbed and clean, at least until recess. He obviously was acquainted with soap and water.

She was in her first year as a teacher at Heltonville and was unaware of the customs of farm families who lived around town in the early 1940s. "What do you mean, you don't buy soap?" she asked, now more curious than upset.

Pokey liked center stage. "We make our own lye soap," he explained. "And if my mouth was washed out with that stuff, I couldn't say boo for a week."

The teacher had grown up in the city, spent four years in a college dorm and had never heard of lye soap. "How do you make it?" she asked.

Pokey explained about butchering, about how hog fat, a major ingredient, was rendered into grease in an outdoor kettle over a hot fire. "Mom stirs the lard scraps so they won't scorch, lets them cook for a couple of hours, then dips out the pieces which by then are cracklings. That leaves only the grease. She— Mom that is—pours in enough lye for a half-and-half blend. She then stirs the mixture, slow-like, but continuously, to make sure the grease and lye mix.

"I don't know how, but she usually can tell when a batch is about finished. She knows for certain when she dips a chicken feather into the kettle. If only the quill is left when she pulls it back out, the soap is done. And plenty strong since it has devoured the feather."

It was the teacher who was being educated. "What then?" she asked.

Pokey shifted his feet as he stood beside his desk. "Then," he said, "Mom pours about three inches of the mixture into the bottom of cardboard boxes and waits for the liquid to set. When it does, it is hard, gold like in color, smelly, course, and strong enough to take axle grease out of knuckle creases. The soap is then sliced into bars, which are bigger and heavier than Lifeboy."

The teacher was learning more than she wanted about lye soap. "It must be strong," she said.

Pokey had some allies by then. "That's why none of us junior high boys has pimples," Bogey laughed. "But thick skin," added Tad.

The teacher ended the discussion. Pokey opened his book to the page she mentioned, but not before scribbling a note he passed across the aisle to Bogey.

"Bet that's the last time she suggests I have my mouth washed out with soap," it read.

News Of The Day

Bugsy hung his Mackinaw jacket on a hook at the back of the classroom, laid down a newspaper and told his buddy, Tad:

"Things aren't going to be nearly as exciting around our house from now on."

Tad had no idea what he meant. Bugsy quickly explained, nodding toward the newspaper, the name at the top identifying it as the Bedford Daily Times-Mail. The month was February, the day forgotten in time, the year 1942.

"Instead of two papers, Bedford now has just one," he said. "The Daily Times and the Daily Mail have merged."

Tad, whose parents had taken the Daily Mail, wondered what the merger of newspapers had to do with the amount of excitement at Bugsy's home.

"A lot," Bugsy explained. "My dad is a big Republican and he read about every thing in the Daily Mail, said its word was as dependable as the Bible, which Mom often doubted. She is a Democrat and she liked the Times, because it ridiculed the Republicans.

"About every night Dad would sit by his coal oil lamp and read the Daily Mail. Mom would sit by her lamp, knit a while, then read the Times."

Tad looked interested.

Bugsy continued his dialogue. "Dad would find some anti-Democrat item and read it out loud to Mom, laughing as he did. She would get upset until she found a story that made the Republicans look bad, read it to him and add, 'So take that.' They acted like they were angry at each other, but Dad would usually wink at me so I'd know the spats wouldn't lead to divorce."

Tad's father was more anti-Democrat than Republican, which explained why he had preferred the Daily Mail. His mom never mentioned politics, didn't even admit how she voted, so he recalled no such arguments between his parents.

The teacher overheard Tad and Bugsy. When the bell rang, she discussed the merger of the two papers to the class.

The Times, she said, had praised every Democrat, vilified each Republican who was in office or sought to be. The only good Republican, it thought, was a defeated one.

The Daily Mail, she added, was surly, even vicious, toward Democrats.

"I remember," she said, "it printed—right on the first page— every morsel of dirt it could find about Paul McNutt when he was governor. And it railed at President Roosevelt, said his social engineering would lead the country into bankruptcy."

"No wonder Dad liked the Daily Mail," Tad thought to himself. His dad detested the government's interference with his life or with his farming, especially when it came to acreage allotments. He blamed Roosevelt and his gang of intellectuals, as he called them, for that.

Tad raised his hand. The teacher nodded. "Which paper did you like better?" he asked.

Being the teacher, she was smart. "I think it's time we turn to our geography lesson . . . and away from politics," she said, ducking the question.

* * *

The U.S. had entered World War II two months before the merger. Bugsy's parents forgot their political differences until the 1944 election, which the Times-Mail covered more fairly than either the Times or the Mail would, had they been separate papers.

Newspapers changed. Political correctness, fairness and balance became guidelines. Bugsy's dad would have preferred the partisanship of the past. Tad's father would have wanted a paper that always agreed politically with him. He'd call any that didn't "namby-pamby."

What's In A Name?

Gordy may have been born with a Webster's dictionary in his mouth. There certainly was no silver spoon.

Gordy was never at a loss for words. It was a good thing for he seldom stopped talking. He added spice to bland conversations, sparkle to mundane discussions. When he talked, the words rolled out quickly, like a boulder down a cliff, rising and falling for accent.

Gordy was among a half dozen junior high boys who had gathered with their lunch pails in the boiler room at Heltonville school one cold March Friday in the early 1940s. It was a place they could laugh, talk loud and be free of classroom confinement for a half hour or so.

The topic of the day turned to farm animals. Tad mentioned "Bossie," one of the cows he had to milk each morning. Tyke talked about currying his dad's team, "Molly" and "Bird."

Gordy said, "I bet none of you name your hogs." He was right. His companions lived on places around Heltonville that were large, envelopes compared to the postage stamp Gordy called a farm. They raised hogs by the truck load. Gordy's dad kept only a few.

"Yep!" Gordy said. "We got names for our hogs. 'Boots.' 'Shirts.' 'Overalls.' 'Shoes.' "

Tad rolled his eyes. Tyke almost choked on his peanut butter sandwich. "Strange names for swine," Cecil said. "How did you come up with them?" he asked.

Gordy, for once, was mum. He avoided an answer.

Instead he pulled a pocket knife from his pocket and used it to pry dried dirt from under the soles that had flopped loose on the clodhoppers he wore. It was the only pair of shoes he had. The twine he had used to keep the soles attached to the toes had decayed in the mire of an early thaw.

"Come on, Gordy," Tad said. "Why would you call a hog 'Shoes?' "

Gordy grinned as the bell rang. "That's a story for another day. I'll let you know later," he said, slamming the lid on his lunch box. Tad forgot about "Shirts" and "Boots" and "Shoes" until a week or so later when Gordy walked proudly into the assembly in a new pair of work boots.

"Tell you about 'em at lunch," he whispered, reading the inquisitiveness in Tad's eyes.

At midday, Gordy crossed his legs to accentuate his new footwear. The shoes had deep tread, a rich, soft leather, not yet spoiled by the scent of the farm.

"You find oil on your land?" Tyke asked. Gordy enjoyed the attention. "Nope," he replied. "Dad sent the hogs to market. Got $7.50 a hundredweight for 'em.

"You see," he said, " 'Boots' brought enough to buy us boys each a pair of shoes. 'Shirts' paid for new denim shirts."

His friends were beginning to get the message.

"Tomorrow I'll wear the Big Macs that 'Overalls' paid for," Gordy added.

Tad shook his head " 'Shirts?' 'Boots!' 'Overalls.' When I get a few years older I'm gonna name about five of our hogs 'Used 1941 Ford V-8 Coupe.' "

Gordy paid him no heed. "Life," he was explaining, "is all a matter of cash flow." And terminology.

A Fire Brand

Miss Clark should have known not to comment on the weather when Gordy was in her English class.

Gordy could turn a chance comment into a personal commentary that lasted until the bell rang. What he hadn't experienced, he could imagine. All he needed to take over a class was a topic.

Miss Clark gave it to him that mid-October morning when she mentioned the overnight freeze had forced her to scrape ice from the windshield of her gray 1939 Plymouth.

"Can I tell you about the fire I built last night?" Gordy asked.

Miss Clark corrected him. "It is may I." She didn't want to stifle a boy's interest in self-expression, for she considered verbal skills as important as written essays when grammar was involved. She nodded for Gordy to proceed, expecting him to talk only for a minute or two.

Gordy, who lived in an old house outside Heltonville, arose, stood beside his arm chair, unabashed, king of the classroom. "Well," Gordy said. He always started his sentences with "well." "I was listening to 'Jack Armstrong, the All-American Boy,' and Mom says, 'Son, it's getting kind of chilly. Why don't you build a fire?'

"Well, we don't have a furnace, just a stove made from an old steel drum with a door welded on the front. It sits on bricks, about this high," he said, holding his hands about 4 inches apart. That had nothing to do with his story, except to prolong it. "A stove pipe goes up about so high into an elbow where another pipe leads to the chimney," he added.

Miss Clark noted that a lot of rural homes had similar heating systems. That didn't bother Gordy. "Well, anyhow, I went out in the wood house and split an old poplar board into thin slivers. I placed that kindling on some newspapers into the stove and set them afire with a kitchen match after adjusting the damper.

"Then I carried in some wood that had seasoned for a couple of years and laid three sticks on the burning kindling. As soon as those sticks caught fire, I added a couple more."

Miss Clark asked, "Isn't that how most of us build fires?"

Gordy looked at the clock on the wall. He had time to kill. "Well, yeah. But let me tell you what happened then. I started doing some home work," he continued, which caused Miss Clark to roll her eyes in wonder because Gordy seldom prepared for class.

Gordy didn't notice. "Well, all at once, my sister yells that the house is going to burn up. The stove had turned from black to orange and the pipes were red from the heat. My sister was crying, 'The pipes are going to melt and drop onto the floor and set the house on fire.'

"I ran into the living room, and saw what she was talking about. There was nothing I could do, except to pray and let the fire burn. Mom wasn't that scared. She took a look at the pipes, said she hadn't meant for me to build a fire that hot and returned to the kitchen to fix supper."

"So what happened?" Miss Clark asked.

"Well, as soon as the wood burned, the stove cooled off and the pipes turned from fire red to stove polish black. I told Dad about it when he got home and he said he'd done the same thing before he learned not to put too much wood in the stove." Gordy paused.

One of the students wondered if the story had a moral.

"Well, I guess if you want a hot time, see me," Gordy said.

Everyone laughed, including Miss Clark. But she never mentioned the weather again . . . not when Gordy was in her class.

Walking The Plank

Chig not only had to toe the line at school, he sometimes needed to walk the plank to get here.

That's why he laughed out loud one morning when the substitute teacher complained about stepping in a puddle of water between the parking lot and the school.

"You needed a foot log," he said.

A few other students snickered.

"It's not something to joke about," the teacher said, "not when a new pair of black shoes have been dyed brown with muddy water." Shoes didn't cost much at the time, but the price took about all a substitute teacher from the city would make in a day.

"Maybe, you'd like to tell the class what's so humorous," she said, a cold stare linking her to Chig.

Chig knew he was in trouble. But he made the most of his plight, being smarter than the average 10-year-old. He explained about planks and foot logs and late winter rains that turned dry gulches into swift currents.

He had walked a plank, he said to get to the school bus that morning. "Actually it was more than a plank. It was a foot log, about 20 feet long, 15 to 18 inches wide," he said.

And he wasn't the only one in class to have done that, he added. "A lot of other kids here at Heltonville have to use foot logs in late winter and early spring after heavy rains."

The teacher was curious by now. "So what is a foot log?" she asked.

Foot logs were common in the hill country, Chig said. "They're bridges that cross cricks that separate homes from county roads. We call 'em cricks, even though we know they're creeks. Truth is they're dry most of the time. They become rampaging streams after a few hours of rain."

Chig was on a roll, like a Christmas tree carried by the current of a flooded ravine. "The cricks take top soil and anything else in their way to Back Creek, White River, the Wabash, the Ohio, the Mississippi and the Louisiana Delta," he said, showing the teacher he knew something about geography.

That's when the foot logs become important, he added. "I couldn't have crossed the creek without one this morning," he said.

The teacher's anger had subsided, like a creek after a flood. "But I still don't know what a foot log is," she said.

By now, other students had turned the dialogue into a class discussion.

No two foot logs were the same, she was told. Some were half logs, the hewn or sawed flat side for walking. Some were two eight by eights, side by side.

"Has anyone ever fallen in?" she asked.

Chig laughed again. "Just when we want an excuse not to come to school."

He was fibbing. "We just learn to balance ourselves," he said, "our lunch buckets in one arm, our books in another. Sometimes, like this morning, the log gets awfully slippery in the rain."

It was something, the substitute admitted, she had never experienced.

"If the road hadn't gone through, you could drive out to my house and walk across our foot log," Chig told her.

The substitute teacher smiled, her mind off her soaked shoes. "What do you mean the road has gone through?" she asked.

That would prove to be a topic for another day.

* * *

"Gone through" was a term rural folks used when spring thaws came and vehicles on stone and gravel on county roads sank through to the mud and mire.

Strangers Arriveth

Six weeks had passed since the strangers had arrived in Heltonville for the first time aboard a little "Polk Township—Monroe County" school bus.

There weren't many of them, maybe 10 or 12, ranging from elementary to high school age.

They had looked as vulnerable as a fire hydrant at a dog convention, as out of place as a farmer in bib overalls at a formal dance.

This, after all, was Heltonville, the buses marked "Pleasant Run Township—Lawrence County." A foreigner was anyone who lived more than eight miles away. The newcomers were alien to the Heltonville students who had spent their school years together, had known each other since the first grade.

Township lines had segregated Pleasant Run from students in Jackson County to the east, Monroe County to the north, Guthrie Township to the south.

Polk Township had no school and the trustee there had decided to transfer what few students there were to Heltonville instead of to Monroe County schools.

It was the late 1930s, maybe the early 1940s. If Pleasant Run was a poor township, Polk was destitute. Few people lived around Chapel Hill, at Yellowstone, up on Dutch Ridge, along Hunter's Creek or up in Dennis Murphy Hollow. The few farms in the township were small, their fields tiny patches between creeks and hills.

Government agents had already begun to buy parcels of the scrub land for the Hoosier National Forest.

It was this background from which the students had come over gravel roads into Heltonville. In days to come, the bus would be muddy from rains, the students' shoes caked with clay.

If they felt out of place, they needn't have. Most of the Pleasant Run students came from homes which were almost as isolated, were nearly as woebegone.

Slowly the newcomers blended into their new environment, lost their reticence, made friends, joined in classroom discussions. All of them, that is, except Roy.

Roy was a hellion, a couple of years older than the other kids in his class, having been held back more for lack of effort than for lack of intelligence. He talked mean, was big and strong, picked a fight almost every recess even if the teacher was watching.

Other sixth graders tried to ignore him, lest they be cajoled into fights they could not win.

Tad talked to his dad one night after Roy had elbowed him against a wall as they ran for the school buses when the final bell rang. "He's always doing something like that," he related.

Tad's father urged understanding. "He may just want some attention. Why don't you, Bugsy, Chig and the other boys try to be more friendly. Let him sit with you when you're having lunch out on the playground or choose him on your team when you choose up sides?"

Tad doubted friendliness would work, but he agreed to try. Roy was skeptical at first, surprised that classmates who had avoided him now sought his attention.

In a few weeks, Roy had changed. Students with whom he had picked fights became his friends. His grades didn't improve much, though.

That was the teacher's job, not Tad's. Roy now had a smile across his face as he waved from his seat on the little bus as it pulled away from school each afternoon.

* * * *

Part of Polk Township later was bought for Lake Monroe and the ground around it became more valuable. What students there are now attend Monroe County schools.

Country Ways

Miss M. had spent the last eight months learning the lifestyles of her rural students. It had been an education for her, being exposed to junior high youngsters who had grown up on farms and knew little about life elsewhere.

She was from the city, wasn't accustomed to their country ways. Now, that school was just a couple of days from summer recess, she still had lessons to learn.

It was the early 1940s and the academic year at Heltonville, like most rural schools, ended in late April. Some parents agreed a student who hadn't learned what he needed to know in 160 days wouldn't be any smarter after 180.

But back to Miss M. She hadn't expected a rebuttal when she told her class, "You are lucky. Schools in Bedford won't be out for three more weeks. The students there will envy you, being able to play and enjoy being outside."

Tad, who never saw a sentence he couldn't dissect, raised his hand. Miss M. nodded.

"You can call it luck if you want. And as far as being able to be outside, well, I'll be outside plenty. So will Gordy, Cecil, Donald and the others," he said, moving his right arm around the class.

He held his long sleeve against already bronzed arms, keeping it from unrolling, then added: "But none of us will be playing and we won't always be enjoying ourselves."

He paused long enough for Miss M. to ask him to explain.

"Well," he said, "now that we're 12, some of us 13, we'll have to work. My Dad says he wants me to turn over a rocky field by holding a walking plow pulled by a team of horses. Says if I can handle that job, he knows I'm responsible enough to drive the tractor."

Miss M. allowed as how that might be a harder test than the ones she'd given.

Tad nodded. He wasn't finished. "After that I'll have to help plant corn, liftin' 80 pound sacks of 2-12-6 fertilizer for days on end, take care of the horses mornin' and night, help with the milkin,' turn the cream separator, beat the rugs when Mom cleans house . . ."

He stopped, looked at Miss M. and said, "You think I could enroll for classes at Bedford."

She joined the class in laughter, knowing he'd rather be caught in knickers than in a classroom in Bedford. She asked, "Will this work go on all summer?"

"There's always something," Tad said. "Pretty soon we'll have to chop the shoots out of the corn in the new ground, put up the first cuttin' of alfalfa, build new fence. Then it'll be time to cut and shock the wheat, help on the threshin' crew, take a scythe to the fence rows, pick tomatoes . . ."

Miss M. had the picture. "I'm sure you won't spend all your time at work."

Tad had taught her that he sometimes dwelled on the negative. He admitted there would be good times, too. "Oh, I'll take a day off to ride to Indianapolis with the trucker who takes our hogs to the stock yards. And there are a couple of county fairs, and the free shows at Norman every Saturday night. Then there'll be ice cream socials and basket dinners at church and watermelons to eat. And on Sundays we usually go for long bicycle rides before spendin' the rest of the afternoon swimmin' in Back Creek."

Tad finally sat down, lest he be too tired to enjoy the things he had planned.

Miss M. thanked him, then added a mental note to what she had been taught by her students: "Good times usually follow bad."

Time Of Transition

Students did not come to study, or teachers to teach, that last day of school.

That didn't keep anyone with eyes to see and ears to listen from observing the inevitability of change amid the familiarity of sameness.

It was the mid-April finish of the 1940-41 academic year, the conclusion of the minimum 32 weeks of classes mandated for township schools.

Much had changed in eight months. War in Europe dominated the news. America was being drawn into the conflict. The nation had begun to build its own fighting machine. Defense plants were in operation.

Factories closed by the Great Depression reopened to make weapons of destruction. Young men were ordered by the Selective Service System to report for induction. Others volunteered for service.

The students at Heltonville had been shocked when coach Cladie Bailey, a reserve officer, was activated a week earlier.

The summer ahead was certain, too, to be a time far different than any the students had known.

That aside, the end of school at Heltonville was much the same as it had been at the close of every year. Girls dressed up, just like they did back in September for the first day of school. Some brought their younger brothers and sisters, a preview to the first grade.

Boys wore the same denim overalls or cotton pants they had worn week after week.

Most students seemed happy. They wore wide smiles, but so did teachers like Mr. East and Miss Clark and bus drivers the students called Buck, Shorty, Goffria and Glenard.

It was difficult to tell which group was the happiest.

Some students weren't that ecstatic, though. A few junior high girls cried, not because they loved school. It was their friends they would miss, friends who lived across Pleasant Run Township. No more than 10 miles would separate them for the summer, but they knew their paths would seldom cross.

They promised to see each other at Fourth of July celebrations at Freetown or in Bedford, but those trips would depend on their parents because most were too young to drive.

Boys and girls, who had grown fond of one another, said their goodbyes, promised to write for there were few phones, except party lines for all to listen.

Older students knew the fickleness of love, that these sweethearts of the past year might find other romances over the summer.

Report cards were handed out. Students turned to the back page, bypassing grades of the last period, eager to see if they had been promoted.

Teachers bid farewell to students; students said so long to teachers.

The final bell rang. Students, except those who lived in town, boarded the buses.

Tomorrow, the girls would remain at home to work in flower beds and gardens and help with house cleaning. Their mothers would be their teachers in a laboratory of domestic science.

Boys would enter the classroom of the outdoors, their subjects nature, agronomy, climatology, horticulture, mechanics, conservation, fence building and farm economy. Their curiosities would be their incentives, their dads their instructors.

It would be the first in a summer vacation of constant change, each day bringing a new development. No one would escape the drama that unfolded.

All, except the seniors, and a few dropouts, would return to school in September much wiser after a summer unlike any before.

Chilled By Fire

News traveled slowly over the hills, across the creeks and up the hollows around Heltonville in 1942.

Which explains why the elation of the last day of school turned to despair for students aboard some of the buses as they creaked into the parking lot that Tuesday morning.

Only a few bothered to leave their seats. Most could see all they cared to from the windows of the buses.

Some of the girls sobbed. A few of the boys turned to hide the embarrassment of their tears. Had there been a radio station in Bedford, a morning newspaper or more telephone lines into isolated areas, the drivers and the students would have known about the disaster which they now viewed.

A fire had destroyed two-thirds of the school, built in three stages over the last 35 years. Now, the first two sections were in ashes, smoldering amid warped steel girders in the basement, part of which had been the gymnasium. The chimney, which remained, towered unsupported over the still-warm rubble.

Trustee Jack Clark and Principal Loren Raines went from bus to bus, explaining the fiery drama of the previous night.

It had been commencement night, a time when the 13 seniors were to receive their diplomas. They had walked onto the stage on one side of the gym, listened to Rev. J. E. Harbin give the opening prayer, waited as the Glee Club stood to sing.

Suddenly Sally Henderson, who lived nearby, ran into the gym shouting, "The school's on fire! The school's on fire!"

Parents, relatives and friends of the graduates fled quickly, but orderly and without panic. The graduates followed. This time there was no processional.

Outside, flames swept across the roof of the first section built in 1907, then spread to the gymnasium/classroom area added in 1925.

Men and boys entered and re-entered the burning building, salvaging records from the principal's office, typewriters and sewing machines from the commerce department, basketball uniforms from the dressing room.

Hundreds of spectators rushed to the school as the light illuminated the sky, hoping to help, the fire too hot for them to do so. The town had no fire department. A pumper truck, firemen Bill Robison and Ralph Williams aboard, arrived from Bedford and quickly laid 1,300 feet of hose to Leatherwood Creek.

They would attempt to save the third section of the building, mostly brick and concrete in contrast to the oiled floors and wooden inner walls of the older parts. They would succeed, remaining at the scene for four hours, long after most of the spectators had gone home, a loss in their hearts, concern on their minds.

Trustee Clark estimated damage at $100,000, promised to work with O. O. Hall, the county school superintendent to determine where classes would be held the following year.

Meantime, the students on the bus were told to return later to pick up their report cards. The diplomas for the seniors had been saved and would be presented, without ceremony, later.

The buses departed. Only the ping of gravel against the floor of the bus, the creak of metal, broke the silence on the bumpy drive to the rural homes.

Delayed By War

Two months passed since fire destroyed most of the school.

It was their youthful expectations that had led Tad and his friends to believe the school would be rebuilt, a bigger gym erected after the fire. They were 12, 13-year-olds who, in their innocence, were unaware of the demands of war.

The superstitious blamed the fire on the fact there were 13 seniors. Realists couldn't agree on the cause. Now it was June and the darkened bricks still laid heaped among twisted metal in what had been the basement. The basketball floor was gone; the rims, void of nets, barely visible among the debris.

Tad and Bugsy had bicycled into Heltonville to once again view the ruins. Their friend Jackie saw them, walked over from his house across the street to greet them.

"Heard anything about a new school?" Tad asked. Jackie shook his head. "No new school. Not now, not next year, not the year after that unless the war ends," he said.

Tad looked stunned, Bugsy shell-shocked. "Come on over home," Jackie said. "I think Mom saved a story out of the paper the other day." His mother pulled a newspaper clipping from a desk to confirm the bad news.

She read: "A drastic government order blocking virtually all new construction work, private and public, except for the war effort, went into effect today.

"The war production board's order prohibited any residential construction other than maintenance and repair work if the cost is $500 or more," she continued, then explained:

"So that means no new school for the duration."

"Duration," they had learned, meant until the war was over. Bugsy wanted to know "how come?"

Jackie's mother read another paragraph: "The board said the purpose of the order is to allocate steel, copper, iron and other scarce materials away from unnecessary construction and into fighting materiel and needed defense housing."

"So where will we go to school?" both Bugsy and Tad asked almost at once.

That, they learned, hadn't been decided. Bugsy and Tad finished the lemonade they'd been given. "Need to get home to help with the milking," Tad said, glumly.

He related what he had learned to his parents. A couple of nights later he rode with his dad to see the township trustee, who told them:

"We'll clean the smoke and damage in the six rooms that still stand, use church basements and rent the Oddfellows Hall down by the railroad. The junior high classes will be in the Christian Church basement," he said, knowing Tad would be an eighth grader.

"In war time, we all have to sacrifice," the trustee said. Until a few months earlier, Tad had thought "sacrifice" was something you did in a baseball game. After six months of war, he'd heard it often, would hear it hundreds of times more in the years ahead.

He had learned to accept the priorities of war. But he did tell his dad on the way home that he had hoped a new school would be built despite the needs of the nation's fighting forces.

His dad said he understood, but added patiently, "Just remember, you learn from teachers and books, not brick and mortar."

* * *

The war lasted three more years. It would take longer—until 1949—for a new school to be built. By then Tad and Bugsy had graduated. What they had learned came not from brick and mortar but from teachers and books.

Smoke Signals

Miss P. had grown accustomed to being corrected by her students. She was in her first year as a teacher, had lived in towns and was unfamiliar with life around Heltonville.

She didn't seem to mind when students disagreed with her. She could, she said, learn from the junior high students and they from her.

That seemed fair enough to Chig. He usually kept quiet in class unless he heard something that didn't ring true. That's why he shook his head and waved his hand one day during a discussion about how Americans communicated with each other.

"The telephone allows us to talk with relatives, friends and neighbors, especially when the weather is too bad to visit," Miss P. said, looking outside where autumn was being overtaken by winter.

She nodded toward Chig.

"We haven't had telephones for two or three years. Lines went bad before the war and my Dad says we'll have to wait until peace comes to have them fixed," he said.

Miss P. wanted to know how they communicated.

"We write letters, sometimes, if the people live a long way off. We just watch for smoke as far as some of our neighbors are concerned."

Miss P. looked puzzled. "Smoke?" she asked.

"Right! Smoke signals," Chig explained.

The class laughed. "Maybe, you'd better explain about smoke signals," Miss P. commanded.

"Go ahead, Tonto," Ralph chuckled. Chig responded, "Well, there are a lot of old people out where we live. Men like Ben and Saul and their wives. Widows like my Grandma J. They can still take care of themselves, but that doesn't stop their neighbors from worrying about them, especially when it gets cold. In warm weather, we usually see them in their yards and gardens."

Miss P. moved from one foot to the other. Chig went on. "They tend to hibernate in the winter, going outside just to bring in wood for their stoves. That's where the smoke signals come in."

Miss P. looked puzzled.

"Well, they're not smoke signals like Indians use. Just smoke. If we see smoke coming out of chimneys, we know people like my grandma and neighbors like Ben and Saul are all right."

Miss P. smiled. "So the smoke really is a signal."

Chig said, "It lets us check up on neighbors. Works almost as good as a telephone," he added.

Miss P. smiled, adding another item to her mental book of folklore.

The Paper Trail

Don always seemed to know more about what was going on in the world than anyone in his class. He always had the answer when the teacher asked a question about current events.

His knowledge was a bit mystifying for he had no more sources of information than any other student at Heltonville. His folks lived out in the country and listened to Lowell Thomas read the news each evening, just like other families in that school year of 1941-42.

But Don knew more than what he could absorb during a 15-minute radio broadcast. His awareness baffled Tad, as well as his teachers.

"How come you know so much?" Tad asked, bluntly, one day.

Don wasn't as quick with an answer as he usually was. He was more indirect. He suggested instead that Tad watch him the next day at lunch.

It was in the days before school cafeterias. Students brought their lunches in an assortment of containers. Some carried their food in paper grocery bags, some in rectangular tin boxes with handles on rounded, hinged lids that contained thermos bottles.

Others had erect cylinder-like boxes with wire handles on top. A cup with soup could be lifted out so the sandwiches could be removed. Some students from poorer families carried gallon pails with tops.

Students from wealthier families had fancier lunch boxes, 8 inches square and 3 inches deep with drawings painted in bright colors on the top and sides.

Tad had always been too hungry to pay much attention to others. Now his eyes scanned the room, observant as they moved toward Don, eager to learn his secret to knowledge.

Some students removed lunch meat, peanut butter or sausage sandwiches. Cecil bit into a sandwich, fattened by tenderloin strips, fresh from butchering. A few kids who lived in the hills had no meat between homemade biscuits.

Don held up a newspaper wrapped around his lunch and bound with twine. He opened the package, removed two sandwiches and folded the newspaper so he could read it.

He did not talk, as the other students did. Instead, he read the news of the day, rearranged the paper from time to time to look at the sports pages, the comics, even the farm market report.

He was still reading when some of the students pulled on their coats and walked outside to spend the rest of the noon break.

Tad now knew Don's secret.

That night Tad placed his lunch box on the kitchen table and told his mom, "I don't need this anymore. Just wrap my lunch in today's newspaper and tie it with rubber bands or string."

Different Goals

Most students tried to step inside the circles others had drawn, tried to become part of the crowd.

A few didn't care to be pigeon-holed, to be categorized as athletes, rowdies or waiting to be 16.

Walter, Eugene and Maurice were like that. They seemed more independent, less dependent on the need to be accepted, to be in the center of conversations.

Eugene, who lived in town, and Walter, who lived at the end of a bus route, were in the same grade, the class of 1942 at Heltonville. Maurice was younger, a country boy who had his sights on goals higher than the rim on a backboard.

Eugene was Gene, never "Geno." Nobody called Walter "Walt" or Maurice "Maury." Nicknames didn't fit their purposes in life.

They didn't loaf at the pool rooms or hang out in the gymnasium or the restaurant in town. They didn't go out for the basketball team, or even go to all the games.

About the only time Walter and Maurice were seen by other students, it seemed, was on a school bus or at school. It was in the classroom where they excelled, where they earned the praise of teachers and the respect of students less inclined to be scholars.

Oh, they weren't perfect. And they weren't above creating a little mischief now and then. They probably wouldn't have sneaked a smoke or sipped a beer. But they weren't smug or standoffish. They were just more independent, more self-assured than others their ages.

What brought them to mind—50 years later—was a story about Walter in the Bloomington Herald-Times. Walter had retired, an obstetrician and gynecologist who delivered 8,000 or so babies in a 45-year career. Dr. Walter Owens, a man who had spent his life helping others.

Suddenly, the memory spool rewinds to those days in the early 1940s, those hours Walter spent reading on his long ride to school, hours others had wasted in meaningless conversations.

The mind shifts to Eugene, the student. The man who grew up to be a preacher, the evangelist, the Rev. Eugene Dulin who took Christ to millions and made certain some of the Soviet people had Bibles to soothe their souls until communism died.

Walter and Eugene, make that Dr. Owens and Rev. Dulin, two boys in a class of 13 students, who made a difference for a nation and for part of the world.

Then there is Maurice, the hard scrabble farm boy, the Purdue graduate, the Maurice Horton, the Phd. who headed the South Dakota State agronomy department. The man who did so well he moved on to the U.S. Department of Agriculture in Washington.

None of the three would ever boast of what they had accomplished.

They don't need to. Success is its own reward.

PART V

Wins and Loses

The "Country Bumpkin Gang," looked forward to the basketball season, perhaps with as much anticipation as Noah's wait for sunshine. It was more than a game, it was friendly combat, fought in barn lofts, on playgrounds, in gymnasiums.

Games were social events, uniting communities on Friday nights, allowing fans to forget for a time depression, war or whatever the concern of the time and the hour.

Each hamlet with a high school and at least five boys had a team. Games were played in cracker-box-size gyms with few seats, standing room only, crowds toeing out-of-bound lines.

Fans were rabid, their disdain for the opposing team matched only by their disgust with referees.

The gym at Freetown looked like a barn, seats in stall-like recesses off the playing floor. At Smithville, students perched on the stage at one end and rocked the backboard when the opposition shot. The team seldom lost at home. Few schools had showers and visiting teams often dressed in classrooms, or in a band room as was the case at Clearspring.

Those gyms, no matter how small, were envied by the "Country Bumpkins," especially after the Heltonville gym burned in 1942. The war, and gasoline rationing, that came with it, caused the school to cancel its 1942-43 season.

From 1943 to 1949, players from Heltonville practiced at nearby Shawswick and played all games on the road. A home gym, of any dimension or shape, would have been a luxury.

The "Blue Jackets" called themselves the "Gymless Wanderers," which was good because they were far from "wonders."

Players looked forward to the county tourney in January, the sectionals in late February, events played in the 4,400-seat Bedford gym. County schools, which had been rivals during the season, united in their opposition to Bedford and Mitchell, big schools in comparison. Once the bigger schools had won the sectional, however, the "Country Bumpkins" switched their support and became their backers until they, too, were beaten.

A Brighter Season

Winter 1943 had been long, dark, filled with uncertainty, empty of pleasure. Spring had never been more welcome to Tad and his eighth grade friends.

They had endured a winter without basketball, a season canceled when the gym at Heltonville burned and gasoline rationing prevented an entire schedule of road games. They saw no regular season encounters, knew only what they had read in newspaper sports sections blanketed among pages of World War II news.

Now spring had returned to green the grass, to burn off the gloom that hovered over Tad, Tyke, Pokey, Bogey and their companions.

They had seen their first basketball game of the 1942-43 season on the Saturday afternoon of the sectional at Bedford. They had been a losing chorus as they cheered for the county teams against the city Stonecutters.

But they were not disturbed when Bedford won the sectional, as it usually did. It would be their team, their horse to ride, until the tournament trail ended.

They had been amazed at the ability of Bedford's John Brennan, a big center in the days when 6 feet 4 was giant in size. They had been elated when the Stonecutters won the regional, then defeated Evansville Central, 36-25, and Jasper, 46-29, in the semifinals at Vincennes.

And they had scoured the news, seeking every word written the week before Bedford faced Lebanon in the first game of the state finals in the Coliseum on the State Fairgrounds at Indianapolis.

Their parents had to suggest, more than once, that they do their chores, finish their home work before memorizing the basketball stories they stacked on kitchen tables.

Tuesday, Wednesday, Thursday, Friday passed as slowly as the days before Christmas. Now it was Saturday and Tad and Tyke had convinced their dad to buy a new dry cell battery for the radio, there being no electric lines in that farm area.

They listened as the announcers gave the starting line up for Lebanon, Houser, Agan, Mount, Laflin and Truitt. And for Bedford, Wagner, Bellush, Brennan, Simmons and Beretta.

Only the static interrupted their concentration.

Brennan countered each Lebanon basket until Joe Hunter came to his aid with a couple of baskets late in the game. Tad and Tyke sat erect, rigid, unmoving. Neither cheered, lest they drown out the action that came from the radio.

The scoring stayed close, the game well played, suspenseful. Either team could win, the announcers said. The game went into the last minute, still undecided.

"It's over," the announcer shrieked. "Lebanon wins, 36-35."

The boys slumped back into their seats, recalling each missed basket, each unsuccessful opportunity to score. Brennan had netted 21 points to earn selection to most all-state teams. (He would later become an all-American at Notre Dame).

Tad and Tyke listened less intently to the second game; again were disappointed when Batesville lost to big city Fort Wayne Central, a team that would defeat Lebanon that night for the championship. The boys turned off the radio and walked outside.

Their dad noticed their disappointment. "If you can't stand to lose, don't get into the game," he told them again, as he often had.

They nodded, went to a storage shed, removed their baseball gloves, a bat and a ball. It was spring, the sun was out, winter was now only a memory. Basketball season was over. It was a time for a new game to begin.

Stained Image

Bugsy didn't seem too eager, for some reason, to get dressed for that first practice of the basketball season.

It was out of character for him. As a freshman and sophomore he had almost jumped into his trunks and shoes and raced onto the floor, leaving everyone else behind.

Now it was another October 1 in the mid-40s. Bugsy lingered on a bench in a corner of the locker room.

"Got any knee pads?" he asked Frankie, the student manager. Frankie shook his head. It was too early for injuries and floor burns, so he had none available.

Tyke, already voted team captain, stuck his head around a locker. "Hey, Bugs, this is basketball, not meditation," he yelled, friendly like. "Better get your rear end in gear."

Bugsy followed Tyke out on the floor, his hair parted neatly, his shoe laces ivory white, his satin uniform motherly pressed. But that wasn't unusual. He was always well groomed, especially for a boy of 16 who lived around Heltonville.

Had he been given to dishevelment and sloppiness, no one might have noticed his knees, or hooted, if they had.

"Is that a disease or dirt?" Billy asked, eying Bugsy's knees and lower legs.

"Looks like you've been down on your knees in twin cow piles," Jake observed, "except I don't smell anything."

Bugsy's embarrassment paid the price for their entertainment. He had expected a bit of ridicule and he laughed, hesitantly, with them. "I was hulling walnuts, the other day," he explained.

"Didn't notice my knees were in the hulls until it was too late. By then the stain had soaked through my overalls and covered my knees and legs. Figured homemade lye soap would take off the stain, but it just made it darker."

Tyke said, "Time will take it off."

"If I live that long," Bugsy replied. "Just hope it's gone before the first game or I'll really be embarrassed."

He had created an opening for the team joker. "It wouldn't be the first time you embarrassed the team," Pokey said.

Bugsy joined in the laughter. Coach Gilstrap called for order. A few practices and he would learn his team was more comic than athletic, but this was a new season and there was always hope for improvement.

He offered one tip for Bugsy: "Use the tractor the next time you want to hull walnuts. Drive the tractor tires over the walnuts, then let the hulls and the walnuts dry. When you pick the walnuts up, the hulls won't stain your hands or your knees."

It was time for practice to begin.

* * *

A month later, Heltonville opened the season with a victory over Williams. By then the walnut stain had disappeared. Bugsy's basket with time running out gave his Heltonville team a 25-23 victory.

Coach Gilstrap gave each player a quarter for a sandwich and soft drink when they stopped in Bedford en route home.

Bugsy ordered, not one sandwich, but two; not a soft drink, but a milk shake, using his own money to pay the extra charge.

"A rich uncle die?" Len asked.

"Nope! I just sold my walnuts last night," he replied, patting his left rear pocket to make sure his billfold was secure.

One L Of A Trick

They were brothers with the same initial for first names too long to fit in the newspaper box scores.

That's why Al Brewster, sports editor of the Bedford Daily-Times, decided to use "B." and "L." when he typed the box scores.

"B." identified the bigger, and older brother, "L." the younger, smaller one. B. was a better, more experienced player as a junior, than L. who was a sophomore.

Enough background! This isn't a story about initials but about the brothers. B. was a starter, a star if anyone on the seldom victorious 1944-45 Heltonville team could be called a star. L. was a reserve who came off the bench when—and if—the coach decided to make a substitution.

Wilbert Gilstrap was coach only because most men who wanted to be were at war, fighting in the Pacific or in Europe. He tried, but acknowledged he was more of a traffic cop, sending players in and out of the game. Trouble was, in L.'s mind, he didn't always send him into the game as often as he should.

That changed one night in January when Tad decided he'd spent enough time gathering splinters. He watched as a referee signaled a foul on brother B., leaned over and said to the coach, "That's his third. Better let me go in and get him out of the game before he gets a fourth."

"Okay," the coach agreed. "Just make sure you know who your man is."

On the bench, B. fumed, demanded to know why he had been taken out of the game. "Three personals," the coach said. "Two," said B.

"L. told me it was three," the coach insisted. By then B.'s face was redder than the red in the uniform of the rival Tunnelton Indians. "I'll kill him! I'll kill him!" he threatened.

"Go back in," Gilstrap said, wanting to avoid bloodshed.

"Cheap trick, punk!" B. told L. as they passed. "Just miscounted," L. replied, a hint of a smile on his face.

L. waited for two weeks to try the "three fouls" ruse again. This time he picked another player, lest he be a victim of fratricide. The player he relieved was as livid as B. had been.

Gilstrap hid the humor he found in being victimized again. He called on the student manager to keep track of the personals for the rest of the game.

But L. had made his point. The next game Gilstrap wrote the starting lineup in the scorebook. B. was on it, so was L.

"Anyone who wants to play that much deserves a chance to start," Gilstrap said.

L. agreed. B. still wasn't convinced.

Consorting With Enemy

Chig had mixed emotions as he dressed after the basketball game at Freetown.

Heltonville had lost again, by a wide margin as often was the case, but he had played well.

Coach Wilbert Gilstrap looked up from the scorebook and said, "Good game, Chig. You scored 18 points. If you play that well off the bench I may never start you again." Chig couldn't tell if he was serious.

He usually scored in single digits, averaging 6 or 7 points a game, and the coach decided a seat on the pines might cause him to play harder.

The decision made Chig angry, knowing he wouldn't start the game at Freetown. He had become friends with Dean, Bill and Chuck, the Spartans three top scorers and had looked forward since last summer to playing against them.

Chances are, as teens were apt to do, he had exaggerated his role as a player. And now he had been benched, embarrassed by his coach, sure to be the source of taunts from his Freetown friends.

When the game started, he had taken a seat as far away from the coach, fuming about his role on the bench. When Freetown raced to a 14-4 lead, Gilstrap summoned Chig and asked, "Are you ready to play?"

Chig, still upset, replied, "That's why I'm here, sir," accentuating the sir.

He scored almost as soon as he was on the floor, soon found himself open again for a lay up. He was surprised at the Freetown defense for he was seldom guarded. His shots came easy, but his scoring failed to offset his team's deficit.

He was in double figures by the third quarter and continued to get easy baskets as the game wound down. The Spartans, Bill and Dean especially, seemed to make no effort to stop him.

There really was no need. Freetown had a big lead and Bill had scored 35, twice as many points as Chig. By the time the game ended Heltonville had lost by 30 points or so.

Chig accepted congratulations from his teammates and coach and waved to the Freetown players as he walked toward the bus. "Talk to you later," Dean yelled back.

On the bus, Chig wondered if his performance would be mentioned in the Bedford Times-Mail the next afternoon, and whether he'd be back in the starting lineup for the next game, which was against Fayetteville.

* * *

The Times-Mail had no story on the game the next day. Chig would have to wait to see the Brownstown Banner to read a report of the game. He did start the Fayetteville game, didn't play as well, noticed he was guarded more closely than he had been at Freetown.

He saw Bill and Dean, his Freetown friends, a week or so later. It was then that they admitted they had conspired to give him some open shots, let him score baskets he might not otherwise have.

"But you still had a good game," one of them said.

Consorting with the enemy may have been bad in those war-time years of World War II. It hadn't been for Chig.

Game Without Winner

Newspapers from Boston to San Francisco carried the story:

"Indiana high school basketball game ends in a tie. Tunnelton 36, Heltonville 36."

In a moment, the rest of the story. First, some background.

It was February 8, 1946, a time when almost every Indiana hamlet was identified by its high school team. The closer the schools were geographically, the more heated the competition.

Heltonville and Tunnelton were close, 8 or 10 miles apart, across a few hills and hollows, separated by U.S. 50.

Fire had destroyed the Heltonville gym a few years earlier and the Blue Jackets had become known as the Gymless Wanderers, playing all games on the road.

The Tunnelton gym was packed, the three rows on each side filled, leaving fans standing in the corners and at each end. Neither team was having a great season and each saw the game as a chance for a victory.

It was a time before digital scoreboards, clocks that showed time by the seconds, horns that blared over the noise of the crowd. A faint whistle, blown by the timekeeper, was the only signal that time had run out.

The two coaches, Wilbert Gilstrap of Heltonville and Lester Gilstrap of Tunnelton, were brothers, good men who were better teachers than basketball mentors. They had agreed to take over the teams in World War II, and although the fighting had ended, young coaches had yet to be mustered out of service.

It would be a night when brotherly love would exceed the bitterness of a hardwood rivalry.

It was game time! Heltonville took an 8-7 lead at the end of the first quarter and was ahead, 19-13, when Haden Crane of Tunnelton hit from the field as time expired.

Despite protests by Shorty White, the Heltonville score-keeper, and Irvine East, the timekeeper, the basket was counted. White insisted that the clock had run out at least 15 seconds before the officials could stop play.

It seemed unimportant at the time. Heltonville remained ahead, 26-19, when the fourth quarter began. Suddenly the momentum turned. Tunnelton came back to lead 38-36, the disputed basket by Crane the difference.

Time was running out when a Heltonville player hit from the field, a basket that, if counted, would send the game into over-time.

Again an argument broke out. Tunnelton's official scorer and timer claimed the basket came six seconds too late. The Heltonville scorer and timer disagreed.

The referees, unable to detect when the clock had expired, left the decision to the official scorer and timer. Being from Tunnelton, they, of course, waved off the basket.

Tunnelton fans left, thinking the Indians had won.

Wilbert Gilstrap sent the Heltonville players to the dressing room. He, brother Lester, and the timers, scorers and referees went into a conference.

The players dressed quickly, it being a time before small schools had showers, and boarded the bus. They waited and wondered for 40 minutes before coach Wilbert rapped on the door.

"What happened?" a dozen players asked in unison.

"We've decided to call it a tie game," he said, explaining that neither Crane's basket at the half nor the Heltonville shot at the end of the game would count.

There would be no overtime, no replay, he said.

"A tie game," one player shouted. "That ought to make the papers tomorrow."

Coach Gilstrap disagreed. "We decided not to report the game," he said, "we" being he and brother Lester. He didn't explain the reason for the news blackout, but the players assumed it was to maintain harmony in the two towns.

Tunnelton players also were told the game was a tie.

The Heltonville bus headed northwest toward Bedford. Four players talked among themselves, agreed it was a story too good to be left untold. They asked Gilstrap for the scorebook, noticed the Tunnelton score still added up to 38 and erased two points from Crane's first-half total.

At Bedford, they eased out of the restaurant where the team had stopped, walked a block to the Bedford Times-Mail office and opened the book for sports editor Al Brewster. "Tie game," they told him.

Brewster knew a good story when he saw one. He copied the box score and headlined his report the next day: "Scoreboard error results in tie basketball contest."

Meantime, both the Associated Press and United Press had picked up the story.

It wasn't until the following Tuesday that Tunnelton fans disputed the story. Clifford Flinn, the timekeeper and scoreboard operator, informed Brewster:

"The reason for the tie was that after the game, the referees, timekeepers, scorekeepers and coaches met. The Tunnelton referees and timekeepers said there was no doubt but that Tunnelton won. The Tunnelton coach said, 'In order to have no hard feelings we will just call it a tie.'

"That's where the tie came in."

Flinn's comments left Brewster wondering: "How come they decided to call the game a tie if the referees and timekeeper said Tunnelton won? And how come the Heltonville scorebook had the two teams each with 36 points, 14 field goals and eight free throws?"

Brewster's column remained a forum for debate for three more days, the two coaches remaining silent, above the fray. It mattered not to them, it seemed, who won or who lost. Brotherly love had triumphed over competition.

The two teams remained in the spotlight for a week, ending complaints that Brewster sometimes neglected county teams while covering the Bedford Stonecutters.

The situation had changed. Tunnelton and Heltonville had received statewide recognition for a week. The Stonecutters had been rarely mentioned.

* * *

POSTSCRIPT: Al Brewster never revealed who brought the Heltonville scorebook to his office. If Wilbert Gilstrap suspected the players who did, he never mentioned it to them. When players from Heltonville and Tunnelton meet, even now 50 years later, they still consider the game a tie. It had been more intoxicating than a victory.

PART VI

Road of Life

Most of the trips through life the "Country Bumpkin Gang" took were over roads less traveled.

Highways, which actually were more like lanes, meandered around hills and across hollows. Few followed section lines that marked 640 acre squares. Some made 90-degree turns without warning. Only state highways were paved.

Men knew the roads and were familiar with every resident within five miles. They assumed anyone else was, too.

They identified locations by family names, roads by characteristics. Clearspring Road was called Powerline Road, because it followed a transmission line. Back Creek Road, paralleled the path of the creek, but some men referred to it as Possum Holler Road because of the opossum population.

Motorists from town sometimes were confused by the turns and twists of the unmarked roads. Farmers were always eager to give directions. Such as they were.

Lost Cause

An overnight rain had left the hills, hollows and fields glistening in the sun.

For rural folks around Heltonville, it was a time to enjoy, a respite in a world driven to turmoil by men like Adolf Hitler and Benito Mussolini. For older couples, who lived in town, it was a day to tour the countryside, to drive as far as World War II gasoline rationing would allow.

Wes had written a letter, probably to his oldest son who was at war, and was raising the flag on his rural mailbox when Clancy pulled his old Chevy to the side of the road. The two men were eager to exchange crop reports, now that the corn and soybeans were seeded and the tomato plants were in the ground.

They leaned against the car as they talked, thanking their Maker for the showers that had come at an ideal time.

Clancy's son Bugsy bided the moments, using an index finger to print his initials on the dusty dash.

A car slowed, then stopped beside the men. It was obvious the driver was citified, likely from Bedford or Seymour, Bugsy surmised. He had on a dress shirt—maybe one left over from his days as a merchant—and his wife, or whomever the woman beside him was, wore a store bought dress.

"Thought we'd catch the spring blossoms before they're gone," the man said. "But we're lost," the woman admitted. The man looked embarrassed.

"Where was it you wanted to go?" Clancy asked.

The man replied, "The missus here remembers going to Liberty Church for a revival and she'd like to see the place again. If we can find it, that is."

Bugsy listened, tried to record the dialogue, which he knew would be in detail. He had heard farmers give directions before.

His dad looked at the man. "It's easy. You go up here to the Holland corner and turn left. Go about an eighth of a mile and turn right. You'll pass Ben Kindred's place.

"Stay on that road past Raymond Dodds' farm. Get ready to slow down 'cause the road gets as thin as a tooth pick and as crooked as a dog's hind leg. It winds down a hill, halfway up from Back Creek, halfway down from the top."

Clancy paused and Wes took over. "Then you'll cross over a one-lane bridge and go up another hill that's so windin' you almost come back to meet yourself. When you get to the top, go about a half mile until the road jogs left. Well, it don't really jog, it just turns left 90 degrees there at the Smithwick house, and goes by Campbell Horton's farm.

The stranger looked perplexed. The "missus" cooled herself with a fan, the kind funeral homes gave to churches. The fan had Scriptures on one side. Bugsy smiled, thought to himself, "I betcha she hopes Heaven can help her now."

Any confusion the man showed didn't bother Wes. "Go about a quarter mile and turn right," he continued, then added, "actually, you don't have any choice, 'cause that's the only way the road goes."

Clancy added, "Yeah! On the left you'll see some woods where we have picnics once in a while. Go past the woods until you get to Sears Crossroads. Turn left there at Andy Sears' place and you'll find Liberty about a half-mile up the road on the right. That's on the east side."

The stranger looked at his "missus." She gave him a blank look. He was more confused than ever; had no idea where Holland corner was or where Ben Kindred, Raymond Dodds, the Smithwick House, Campbell Horton or Andy Sears lived.

He eyed the gas gauge, glanced at the "A" gasoline rationing sticker on the windshield of his car and explained: "Maybe we won't go up to Liberty after all. How's the best way to get to U.S. 50 from here?"

Clancy pointed west. "Well, go that way until you get to Hunter's Crossroads, turn left, then make a right turn at Johnny Cummings, a left turn at John Harrell's and . . . "

The man muttered a thanks and started the car. "The missus" was fanning faster than ever as they drove off.

Wes and Clancy, a good deed done for the day, resumed their conversation.

PART VII

Zeke The Man

If the "Country Bumpkins" sought a model from which they could mold their lives, it might have been Zeke.

Zeke was a nickname his sons gave him. He didn't mind, especially since they always called him Dad when other men were around. Zeke was born in 1888, had paid for his farm through his own efforts, caring for crops by day, working at the stone mill at night when he needed extra cash. As a teen, he had traveled to Iowa by horse and buggy, spending the winter shucking corn for a few cents a bushel.

He had seen the automobile replace the buggy, tractors put horses to pasture, combines make binders and threshing machines obsolete, marveled at movie picture shows, gazed at machines in the sky that proved man could, indeed, fly. He was slow to change, leaving others to experiment with the new, waiting to make sure the present was better than the past.

He saw, despite years of delay, rural electrification reach his farm, light up his part of the world and make coal oil lamps and lanterns obsolete.

He was a Type A personality before the term was invented. He worked hard, expected his sons to, and had no tolerance for those who did not strive to be the best they could be. He refused to accept government handouts and damned those who did, switched from Democrat to Republican when Franklin Roosevelt was in office and never forgave him for his social engineering.

Zeke had stored in his memory bank six decades of history, eager to share his experiences with youngsters who might learn from them. They listened to his stories, but they learned more from observing Zeke the farmer and Zeke the man.

Soil Steward

Zeke had the good fortune to farm at a time that was right for him.

He would have snorted at the way farmers operate today; smirked at no-till planting, laughed at commercials for herbicides and pesticides.

Zeke liked the land, held the soil in his hand as if it were gold, cared for it much like others protected their jewels. He farmed back in the 1940s, a time when a man could make a living on 160 acres. All he needed was a Farmall H that pulled twin 14-inch plows, a disk that would pass through a farm gate and a few other implements.

He used the tractor to prepare the soil, plowing seven inches deep, the moldboard rolling over sod so slick the sun glistened off it; disking and harrowing until the dirt was silt so fine it sifted through his fingers. When the field was ready, he'd park the tractor. It was time for the team, Molly and Bird, to go to work.

Other farmers used their tractors to pull corn planters. Zeke wouldn't hear of it. "Tractors pack down the ground too much," he said. "No point in working a field into a silt-bed, then smash it down," he argued, even though he could have planted his fields in half the time.

"Got plenty of time," he'd say, reminding anyone who questioned his wisdom that "Rome wasn't built in a day." Those who heard him say it laughed, for it was about the only time he worked in low gear. When it came to farming he was usually in overdrive.

No matter. He felt good as he pulled a wagon loaded with bags of 2-12-6 Happy Farmer fertilizer and seed corn to an end of the field, then returned to the barn for the horses and planter.

At the field, he filled the fertilizer boxes, then the seed corn boxes on the two-row planter. He pulled down the marker blade that would indicate where to drive the team on the return trip across the field.

The horses stepped off at the cluck of his tongue, their feet sinking below the white on their hooves into the soft earth. They walked straight and true, responding to each gentle command Zeke gave with the reins.

He stopped only to add fertilizer and seed and for lunch, when he spent more time watering and feeding the horses than he did for his own nourishment.

It was a routine that continued for several days, interrupted only by rain. Once all the fields were planted, he'd wait for the seed to germinate, eager to see if the stand was good, that there were no stretches where seed had failed to drop from the planter.

He seldom was disappointed. In a few weeks, he would cultivate the fields with his tractor, sometimes chop out any weeds that grew in the rows. And he would be proud as he watched the dark green blades wave in the breeze that hinted of showers needed to quench the soil's thirst.

The crop would, he reasoned, yield enough to fatten all the pigs his sows would farrow, with a few truck loads left over to sell for cash to an elevator.

Zeke quit farming before it became a big business in which only the strong endure; where time is money and minimum tillage and chemicals are necessary for survival.

He might, with outbursts of profanity, have adjusted to the changes. But he wouldn't have been as happy as he was sitting on that horse-drawn corn planter each May.

No Ladies' Day

Adolf Hitler, the Third Reich, hog prices, baseball, the new preacher . . .

There was no end to the topics farmers could discuss when they visited each other for dinner after church on Sundays around 1940. They weren't afraid to wrestle with, or debate, any problem.

It didn't matter how much they knew about the subject in question. Knowledge could be a hindrance, facts could limit opinion.

It was a game they played for the gratification received from turning words into thoughts, of formulating ideas to generate controversy. It was a form of mental gymnastics that fertilized their minds and kept them from dozing off after dinner.

And it would have been easy to fall asleep that September Sunday when three couples visited Millie and Zeke for dinner. Millie had served chicken and dumplings, roast beef, an assortment of vegetables from her garden and peach cobbler.

Zeke had the afternoon scripted. He led the men into the sitting room, eased himself into his rocking chair and said what he had rehearsed: "Labor Day's tomorrow. Guess we'd better remember to kiss the ground John L. Lewis walks on."

Lewis was the bushy-browed boss of the mine workers, the man who headed the CIO.

The mention of Lewis caused Johnny's face to turn red. He was an individualist who preferred to make his own way in life. A farmer was his own boss, his own hired hand, and he liked the independence. He did not care for Lewis or his unions.

Zeke, at times, worked nights at the stone mill, farmed by day, and had learned both labor and management had viewpoints worthy of consideration.

He was outnumbered. Clem and Joe sided with Johnny. "We never heard of overtime pay, 8-hour days or 40-hour weeks until John L. and his likes came on the scene," Johnny roared.

Zeke snorted, appearing to defend Lewis. "You ever been a mile down under the ground diggin' coal?" He knew his guests hadn't.

He used his favorite phrase to make a point. "You're born, but you ain't dead yet." That meant they still had some learning to do.

"That's right! I ain't dead yet, but I know all I want to know about John L. Lewis," Johnny replied.

He looked at his watch, "Milkin' time," he announced, thanking Zeke for the hospitality, grinning to let him know his defense of Lewis hadn't been taken seriously.

The men walked him into the kitchen where the women were snapping a basket of beans. They had already washed and dried the dishes, scrubbed the pots and pans and peeled a half bushel or so of peaches.

Johnny didn't seem to notice. "I'll be up at the crack of dawn tomorrow, Labor Day or no Labor Day. A farmer never gets any time off."

The women bit their tongues to keep from laughing. The men had spent three hours doing nothing but talk. Their wives had worked the entire time. Labor Day to them would be wash day. And all the other days would be days of labor, too.

But they never complained. Complaining was one job they left to their husbands.

Political Contempt

Most farmers around Heltonville had simmered down, the fire that heated their tempers now only ashes.

Except for Zeke. It was Saturday, four days after the 1944 election and he was still fuming. "I can't believe that damned Roosevelt won again," he said, as he waited to swap wheat for flour at Jerry Jones' elevator.

"If we can't vote him out, we just as well have a dictator," Zeke ranted. Most of the other men nodded in agreement, having become disenchanted with FDR in his first term when the government began meddling in farm programs.

Now he had been elected for the fourth time.

FDR was proof, to these dissenters, that familiarity does indeed breed contempt. Clem turned agitator to generate some heat in the elevator. "You guys would miss seeing pitchers of old Franklin D. and his fancy cigarette holder, actin' uppity. Besides, you don't change horses in the middle of a furrow," Clem argued.

Pictures always came out "pitchers" when he spoke. And his reference to changing horses came from a campaign theme that the country shouldn't change presidents in the middle of the war, which, at last, was going well.

Zeke pushed his gray felt hat back on his head. "Presidents don't win wars. Generals—and boys like yours and mine—win wars. Not self-important presidents."

That didn't stop Clem. "You forget that Harry Truman was elected vice president. He's an old farmer who acts about as common as we do."

Zeke snorted. "We all know vice presidents don't do nothin'."

Someone mentioned that Tom Dewey, Roosevelt's opponent, had carried Indiana by more than 80,000 votes. "Just proves we got more common senses than the rest of the country," Zeke said.

Clem switched from agitator to pacifier. "Well, we did elect two Republican senators. Maybe they can keep an eye on the Great White Father." The men had called FDR "the Great White Father" ever since his AAA program started telling them how many acres of corn to plant and how much wheat to sow.

Homer Capehart had won a six-year U.S. Senate term, beating popular Henry S. Schricker, who wasn't permitted to seek another term as governor. Bill Jenner, a Bedford lawyer who had been an Air Corps captain before losing sight in one eye, rolled up a big margin over Cornelius O'Brien for a two-year Senate term.

That didn't give Zeke much comfort. "If they get lost as many times as I did when I visited Washington, it'll take them four years to find where they're supposed to go," he said, recalling a trip he'd made a few years earlier.

"We'll also have a Republican governor, feller named Ralph Gates," Clem said.

Zeke brushed the elevator dust off his pants. "A governor can't do much while a war is going on and a king like Roosevelt is running the country."

Jerry rolled out three bags of flour on a two-wheel cart. Zeke thanked the miller, picked up the flour and headed for his car.

"Roosevelt won't be president forever," Clem yelled.

Zeke turned and replied, "I wouldn't count on it."

****

President Roosevelt died on Thursday, April 12, 1945. Harry Truman, ex-farmer, became president. Government involvement in agriculture started by FDR continues, nine presidents later.

Time Out For Thanks

Perhaps it was the war—and the sacrifices it required—that caused the usually taciturn Zeke to be more expressive than usual that Thanksgiving Day.

He seldom opened a window to his soul, didn't schedule time to ponder the present or the past, think aloud about tomorrow. He was usually too busy with life to analyze it.

Zeke had farmed near Heltonville for years, learning that good eras always follow bad ones. He was an optimist in a time of pessimism. It was 1943, and the outcome of World War II was still in doubt, although U.S. Flying Fortresses were bombing German targets, air battles were being won in the Pacific and ground forces were regrouping in Australia to resume their attack against the Japanese on New Guinea.

Sugar was rationed, so was meat. Shoes were limited. Gasoline use was restricted and those who hadn't used their quota asked themselves each time they crawled into their cars, "Is this trip really necessary?"

Zeke and his sons had spent that Thanksgiving morning shucking corn, cribbing two loads heaped high on the wagon. The horses, still in harness, the bridles removed, were in their stalls, extra scoops of oats their holiday feast.

At the house Zeke cupped his hands in the dishpan, doused his face, dried on a towel made from a feed sack and joined the family that had gathered at the round table, a leaf added to make room for the extra food.

Zeke didn't offer a prayer, suggested instead a moment of silence to reflect on the meaning of the day.

It was Tyke, or maybe it was Tad, who wondered what, in this era of war, there was for which to be thankful.

Zeke said, "More than you realize. We're all in good health. We've got corn in the crib, wheat in the bin, hay in the loft, meat in the smokehouse, wood in the shed, and canned goods in the cellar.

"And we'll have corn, cattle and hogs to market, which will help feed soldiers, sailors and defense workers and bring us some cash. We can be thankful we'll get through another winter, regardless of what happens.

"We may not have turkey on the table, but we have ham and pork because we butchered a hog the other day, we have bread because we had flour ground from wheat we raised. And milk and butter from our cows."

Tad and Tyke didn't respond, knowing he was right.

Zeke went on. "Some folks in town are a lot worse off than we are. They may have running water, electricity and a store down at the corner, but they don't have the home-grown food we have unless they had room for Victory Gardens in their back-yards."

The smile left his face. "And we are far from the battles of war."

Tyke added some gravy to his potatoes. Tad savored the fresh ham. The conversation continued, interrupted only by a "please pass" now and then until Zeke was ready for slices of the pumpkin and apple pies.

"And we can be thankful your mom squirreled away enough sugar to bake these pies," the grin again spreading across his face.

"Amen!" Tad added.

Zeke pushed his chair back after about 45 minutes. "Time to get back to the corn harvest," he announced firmly lest there be any protest. Neither Tad nor Tyke complained. To do so would ruin the day's significance.

They could be thankful their dad had given them reasons not to sit and whine.

Government Checked

Zeke didn't care for President Franklin Roosevelt, his Agri-cultural Adjustment Act, or anyone who worked for it.

That's why AAA workers dreaded stops at his farm east of Heltonville. They knew he'd be about as cooperative as a rattle-snake cornered in a hen house.

He wasn't the only farmer who detested the AAA's acreage allotments, price supports and other programs. He was the most vocal, and descriptive, in his comments, though.

Zeke was a fierce individualist who didn't ask the govern-ment for help and didn't want it meddling in his affairs. When he needed extra cash, he'd work the night shift at the limestone mill. That made him even more resentful of farmers who seemed eager to accept handouts from Washington.

"First time I ever heard of getting paid for not doing some-thing," he'd rant. "A brotherhood of fools," he called farmers who accepted government checks.

"If this keeps up they'll be expectin' chunks of gold to fall overboard from heaven and looking in their kids' Crackerjack boxes for diamonds."

He roared so loud the rafters in the farm house creaked when he read about the size of some checks big farmers were receiving for not planting crops on part of their land. "Two thousand one hundred and ninety-seven dollars," he bellowed, stretching out the numbers.

"The less you do the more you get," he shouted. That was, he figured, $183 a month and it had been paid to one of the most prosperous farmers in Lawrence County.

"Hell," he screamed, "men are working for the WPA at hard labor for $48 a month. And I get $26.67 for 40-hours a week when I cut stone at the mill."

Had that new unsuspecting AAA worker known about that outburst he might have skipped Zeke that February day. It would have been easier to have faced a fire-breathing dragon.

The government agent laid out the aerial maps of Zeke's farm, the acreage marked on each field. Zeke looked over the maps. "Ain't none of that information right," he snorted. "Them maps are as useless as blankets for pigs."

The government agent cleared his throat. "Our figures don't lie," he said.

Zeke thundered, "I've been farmin' them fields for 20 years and I know how many acres there are in each one of them. I don't need no government agent in a white shirt tellin' me by looking at a map."

The visitor let the maps roll up before stretching rubber bands over them. "Well," he said, "you can't get handouts from the government if you don't sign this agreement showing how many acres you won't plant this spring. Don't be too hasty in turning down a good thing."

Veins grew fat in Zeke's forehead. "Gettin' something for nothin' ain't ever a good thing . . . if it was I'd recommend the government pay you not to stop here and tell me how to run my business."

The visitor left, maps under his right arm. Zeke went to the wall phone and cranked the handle. He asked for the stone mill so he could tell Bill Fuller he'd like to work a few weeks to offset the money he refused to take for doing nothing.

No Luxury Trips

Zeke lived life in the fast lane before there was one. Except when corn planting, he had one speed. All out. If he couldn't do a 30-minute chore in 15, he considered himself a failure.

At the stone mill, where he worked nights, he could out-saw the other operators . . . except when, in haste, he measured wrong and ruined a block. On the farm, he beat his neighbors into the fields each morning where he tried to out-plow, out-plant and out-harvest them.

He often did. Maybe because he slept faster than they did. He was a Type A personality among a cadre of good old boys in no rush to speed through life. All of which helps explain why Tad wasn't surprised when he was given his assignment at the first hay harvest that day in June.

First, though, the stage needs to be set. Zeke had decided to put the alfalfa cutting up "loose" as he called it. That meant it wasn't baled. Instead it was tossed onto a wagon, then taken to the barn where a "fork" was stuck into the hay and pulled by a rope up onto a track from where it rolled across the underside of the roof to a part of the loft where it was to be dropped.

A worker in the mow would yell "dump it." The man on the wagon would jerk the rope, tripping the fork which dropped the hay into the loft.

Most of the time a team of horses or a tractor was used to pull the rope through a set of pulleys at the opposite end of the barn. The driver would know when he heard "dump it" to stop and drive back toward the barn, bringing the rope with him so the slack in it would allow the fork to be pulled back to the wagon more easily.

Back to Zeke and Tad.

"How come you're gonna use the car to pull the rope?" Tad asked, looking at the knot on the front bumper of the 1937 Buick.

"Cause it's a lot faster than the horses or the Farmall H," Zeke answered. "A minute saved is a minute to be used for something else.

"Your job will be to yell for me to stop when you hear 'dump it,' then pull the rope back in front of the car once I start forward. And move fast 'cause we may set some kind of record here today. I figure if Jim can stick that new four-tined grapple hay fork as well as he says he can, we can unload a wagon in six or eight minutes."

Once the two wagons were loaded and brought to the barn, Zeke started the Buick, waited for the signal to go, and sped backwards, as he had promised, at a faster speed than a team or a tractor could. He then drove forward toward the barn even faster once the hay had been dumped.

He had been right. The load was in the barn in less than 10 minutes, the second load in less time. The wagons that followed were unloaded more quickly, even though Tad's arms ached from tugging the heavy rope. He didn't complain. Neither did the man in the loft or Jim who continued to plant the fork so it would cradle big loads.

At day's end, the Buick was coated with the dust Zeke had stirred up once the grass had been worn bare by the Buick's speedy trips. "Looks like your luxury car needs a bath," Jim said as he washed his face in the cold water that flowed from a spring into a pool in the stream.

Zeke looked at the car. "Can't waste time washin' a car. Besides, the rain will take care of that dust one of these days. Anyhow, I just learned a car ain't no luxury. It's a necessity for puttin' up hay."

Hooked On A Peg

Clem and Zeke made good theater when they left their farms for the stages of small towns.

They could be Lum and Abner, Abbott and Costello, or just plain Clem and Zeke, depending on how their unscripted roles developed.

(Abbott and Costello were comedians. Lum and Abner were radio characters supposedly based in Pine Ridge, Ark.)

Clem and Zeke chose the barber shop in Heltonville for their performance that dark, dreary December in early 1940. The audience included a half dozen other farmers who also had been driven indoors by an icy rain.

Joe unsuspectingly raised the curtain on the impromptu performance when he started to leave, saying he had to stop at the Roberts General Store to buy a new shucking hook.

It was a time before many farmers in the area had corn pickers, long before big multi-row gleaners came on the scene. They instead husked their corn crops by hand.

Clem opened the two-man show. "I don't see how anybody can use a hook to shuck corn. I've used a peg, instead of a hook, for nigh on 40 years now and I can shuck as much corn as almost anyone."

Play-acting allowed him to lie.

Zeke bristled, his eyes cuttingly sharp. "Man, I shuck three loads a day and I ain't never seen you crib more than two loads. I use a double hook and no one has ever beat me in a contest using a peg."

The barber wasn't a farmer. "What in the dickens is the difference between a hook and a peg?" he demanded to know.

Zeke explain about a bent hook with a pointed end. "It's a piece of metal attached to a rawhide band that fits over the hand. It has straps that go on each side of the thumb. When the straps are tightened the hook fits snugly in the palm of the hand."

He made a motion with his right arm to show how the hook would cut between the husks and the corn to free the shucks and expose the ear.

"I like twin hooks myself," Zeke added.

Clem spoke up. "I'd turn the hogs into my field before I'd use a hook."

Zeke laughed. "No more than your fields yield, you just as well let the hogs have it," he said.

Clem paid him no attention, explaining, "I have two different pegs. Both have rawhide that fits over two of my fingers, like this. One has a metal peg, tapered at the lower end, the other is wooden and looks like a sharpened dowel pin."

He demonstrated, as best he could without a stalk or an ear of corn, how the peg could be used to rip away the husks.

Zeke groaned. "If I had to use a peg, I'd still be shuckin' at corn plantin' time."

The two men continued their act until Joe stood up and tugged on his fleece lined jacket.

"To heck with a hook or a peg, I'm driving into town to look at one of them one-row International pickers I've seen adver-tised," he said.

Zeke and Clem waited a few minutes and walked next door to the restaurant.

"Good show," Zeke grinned.

"Yeah. Especially since I've never used a shucking peg in my life," Clem said, setting down his coffee cup and looking around to see if there were enough customers to merit another performance.

Corn Cob Syrup

Clem drained the last drip from the maple syrup jar and spread it over the butter atop his biscuits.

It was the last drop in the house. There would be no more until the next February when the sap that flowed from the trees was boiled in the sugar houses in the area.

Clem liked his sweets. He put sugar on toast, even on sweet apple pie. And he likely would be grumpy, his wife knew, without syrup for breakfast.

She would have bought another gallon had it been available. But Mrs. Julian, and other farm families who made maple syrup, had sold every quart the previous spring. The sales gave them extra cash which was in short supply.

Clem was as irritable as she suspected he would be. "Rather do without ham and eggs," he said the next morning. He buttered the biscuits, but not as eagerly as he would have had there been syrup.

In days to come, he would try sorghum molasses, which only soured his disposition. Days passed. Clem's craving for syrup did not.

His wife kept quiet, even that morning when the jar with the retractable lid appeared back on the table. Clem eyed the jar. The contents looked like maple syrup.

"Try it," his wife suggested.

Clem broke open two biscuits, spread a mound of butter over them, then saturated them with the syrup. He took a bite, held it in his mouth to savor the taste, smiled and said, "This is more like it."

His wife evaded a response when he asked where she had found the syrup. He might stay happier, she reasoned, if he didn't know. If he thought it was maple syrup, fine.

A few more days passed. The jar emptied. Clem finished another breakfast, looked at his wife and said, "How many refills do we have left?"

The deception was about to end. "How many bushels of corn do you have in the cribs?" she replied.

Clem looked puzzled. "What in tarnation, woman, does that have to do with maple syrup?"

She walked to her recipe book and pulled out a tattered clipping. "What you've thought was maple syrup has been corn cob molasses," she said. "This is a recipe from an old farm magazine. I just followed directions."

Clem wondered, "How in the world can you get syrup from corn cobs?"

She looked again at the recipe. "I shelled a dozen ears so the cobs would be clean. Then I broke the cobs into small pieces and boiled them for 30 minutes in a half gallon of water on the cook stove. After the water cooled, I poured the contents through the cheese cloth over the strainer."

"Is that all there is to it," Clem asked.

"Not quite," she said. "I added about five pounds of brown sugar. By the way, you'll have to get another bag at the grocer. Then I boiled the sugar in the liquid until I got the right thickness."

Clem reached for more biscuits, which he buttered, then swamped them with corn cob syrup. "No point in scrimping as long as we know the secret, have corn in the bins and enough money to buy brown sugar."

Syrup-making time no longer seemed so far away.

* * *

An addendum: For those who care to test the recipe: Do not stir the brown sugar while the liquid is boiling. It may cause the syrup to become ropy.

Ladies Day Out

Clem steamed, snorted and stewed when Maudie said she was going with him to the feed mill that Saturday morning in March.

He'd be mortified, he said. "Women folk just don't go to the feed mill," he insisted, like a man bent on protecting a male domain.

"I'll be the first one then," she persisted, sort of like a women's rights advocate of the early 1940s.

He wondered "why in the tarnation" she would want to go, anyhow. "Ain't nothin to see but a bunch of dust and feed sacks. Besides, you don't know chicken scratch from pig supplement."

It wasn't the first time she had heard Clem storm. And she fed the chickens morning and evening. And she probably read the ingredient labels on feed sacks closer than he did.

Clem knew it was a disagreement he couldn't win. "Well, let's go," he moaned, "but I still don't know why you want to."

She didn't reply. He didn't utter a word on the 10-mile ride to Bedford. But he did admit, as they walked into the Standish Feed Mill, "I've never been so embarrassed in all my born days."

He look stunned as he looked around the store. Maudie just grinned.

A half dozen other women were there. And they all had their eyes on the feed sacks, an assortment of prints and colors.

Workers looked as perplexed as Clem and the other farmers.

"I knew we shouldn't have spread the word about these new patterns," one said. They knew farm wives, for lack of money to buy items in stores, often make dresses and curtains and towels from feed sack material.

It was obvious it was women's day out. They measured the yards of cloth in a sack with their eyes.

"I'll need four of those bags to make a dress," a woman of size said. Her husband nodded and helped load the sacks into a car.

Another woman found a pattern she wanted at the bottom of 50 other sacks. The teen-ager who worked at the store groaned. But he and a co-worker shifted the feed to free the bags that pleased her.

Maudie's eyes didnt rest until they came to a flowered print. "We need two of those," she said.

Clem was so relieved by then he added, "Better make it three, just to make sure she doesn't run short of material." He didn't bother to check whether it was chicken mash or hog feed. "Don't matter, anyhow," he said. "If the chickens can't eat it, the hogs will."

And he didn't complain when Maudie saw a couple of other sacks she wanted to use for dish towels.

They pulled out of the store parking lot a few minutes later, sacks on each fender, two in the trunk and one in the back seat.

Clem was more talkative on the ride home, even asked Maudie if she wanted to stop for lunch. The trip hadn't been the ordeal he had expected.

It was hard to tell who fared best from that trip to town. The chickens that enjoyed the mash, the pigs that slurped the supplement, Maudie when she modeled her new Easter dress, or Clem who liked what he saw.

Full Service

Clem was surprised his youngsters hadn't said anything to their mother. After all, he had been collecting her Christmas gifts for months.

He needn't have been astonished. For he had made it clear, emphatic, plain, explicit. If they blabbed one word about what he had planned, they would find nothing under the tree for themselves.

His threat might be a bluff, but they took no chances. It was 1940, maybe 1941, and money was scarce as always and any gift would be appreciated.

If Clem had money to spare, he would have waited to buy his wife's present. But he knew there would be little cash to spare when Christmas came.

That's why he started collecting chinaware at the Spur station in Bedford in September. "One piece with each fill-up," the sign at the station promised. And the attendants delivered on the pledge after topping off the gasoline tank, cleaning the windshield, checking the oil and making sure the radiator was full.

It was good service, especially when Clem sometimes stopped when the tank was less than half empty.

Each time, he'd select a piece of china, double checking to see if it matched the pieces he had previously chosen.

He drove into Bedford from his farm near Heltonville more often than necessary, careful not to ask his wife to ride along, lest she accept. One or two of his six children usually joined him when he made the 20-mile round trip on Saturdays.

Now, on the last Saturday before Christmas, he created another excuse to drive to the county seat, knowing his wife was busy making Christmas candy. He parked on the courthouse square while his two sons bought a couple of cheap gifts for their

Sunday School exchange, then headed out I Street to the Spur station.

"Five gallons, $1 dollar," the attendant said. "Need any more china?"

Zeke took a reminder from his billfold. "A saucer," he said.

He again checked the pattern, handed over a dollar and drove off, humming a Christmas melody. "That's it," he told his sons. "I have a set of six plates, six cups and six saucers. My Christmas gift for your mom is complete."

He drove north, turned right on Ind. 58 and stopped at the JayCee store. "Be right back," he said.

He returned with a sack of chocolates with white insides. "Almost forgot I also have a candy dish in that set," he said.

He reminded his sons once again not to reveal his secret.

Dog Had Its Day

Ol Ezra had extended animal rights about as far as he could afford.

Dogs were about to eat him out of house and home. Even his wife, who was too kind to squash a bug or scat a cat out from under her feet, sometimes complained about all the dogs around.

Times were hard enough back about 1940 without a kennel to feed. Ezra had done what he could. More than once, hed taken a beagle bitch named "Dog" a few miles from his home near Heltonville and dumped her out, thinking maybe she would claim some other unsuspecting farmer as her master.

She kept finding her way back, though, wagging her tail as she arrived, rubbing up against the denim pant legs of Ezra's bib overalls. Ezra wouldn't admit it, but a close look would have detected a hint of goodness, like maybe the Lord had forgiven him for his meanness.

His repentance didn't last long. In a few weeks "Dog's" undercarriage would start bulging like an overstuffed suitcase and Ezra would know another litter was on its way.

Ezra just grunted when he learned his wife was fixing bigger meals than necessary, just so she'd have leftovers for the mutts.

He knew better than to take "Dog," expecting like she was, out in the country again. His conscience would have killed him if he had lived through his wife's deathly stares once she found out he was a pregnant dog abductor.

Ezra waited until the pups were born, then fed them all the fresh milk they could drink, hoping to speed their weaning, hasten their orphanage. "No more litters," he swore.

A few weeks later he coaxed "Dog" into a burlap bag, lifted it into the back seat of his dusty old Chevy and headed east.

Winter was coming on and he hoped she would find a new home to adopt. "This time," he told himself, "I'll take her so far she'll never find her way back."

He drove almost to Brownstown, 18 miles or so away, stopped along U.S. 50 and removed the sack, loosening the opening, making sure "Dog" could get out.

He spat a few profanities, attempting to subdue his conscience, turned and headed home. He could see, in the rear view mirror, "Dog" step cautiously from the sack, bewildered at her new surroundings. "No more litters," he thought once again.

He was wrong. Less than a week later, "Dog" was back, licking her young, looking forgivingly at her reluctant master. She knew a dog's best friend was a man named Ezra.

Ezra fixed her a bed of straw in the car shed, knowing cold weather would arrive any day. The next day, he again loaded "Dog" into the Chevy.

This time he drove toward Bedford, carried "Dog" into the veterinarian's office and said: "Need for you to turn this she into an it."

PART VIII

The Slow Lane

Some men merely resisted change. Ben downright resented it. He was ten to fifteen years older than Zeke, never owned a tractor, seldom drove his Model T, the only car he ever owned.

He lived alone with his wife Ellie, perhaps the sole person with whom he really felt comfortable. He didn't bother his neighbors, unless he needed help, which wasn't very often.

Most youngsters ignored him, thinking he was disagreeable, a difficult man, too far removed from his own boyhood to relate to theirs. Tad and Tyke were exceptions, even though, they too, sometimes imitated his gestures and laughed at his old-fashioned habits. But they learned to know the real Ben, a man who appreciated what little he had and refused to move into the fast lane of life.

Every boy should stop on the way to manhood and spend some time with a Ben.

A Christmas Surprise

Smoke scriggled from the chimney of the farm house, forming clouds that rose into the clear, cold December sky.

It was, for Tad, an indication that all was well with Ben and Ellie. He need not have knocked to know that, but he did so, following his mom's request to check on them.

Ben and Ellie were in the twilight of their lives, alone except for neighbors like Tad who checked on them from time to time.

Ben answered Tad's knock, motioned him into the living room and said, "Sit a spell by the stove and warm yourself."

Tad noticed no decorations, no tree, no presents brightly wrapped. The room was the same as it had been throughout the fast-fading year.

Ellie didn't offer him homemade candy or cookies for she seldom baked. She excused herself, picked up the socks she was darning and went into the sitting room, leaving, as she said, "you menfolk to talk."

Talk came easy for Tad when he was with Ben despite the two generations that distanced them. Ben, man wizened by age, encouraged by Tad's curiosity, was eager to impart the knowledge of his years.

"You folks ready for Christmas?" Tad asked.

Ben nodded. "As ready as we'll ever be," he laughed. "When you get our age, Christmas is like any other day, except for the fact it honors Christ's birth.

"We each have everything we need. We've got each other, a place to live, food to eat, wood for fires, some books to read. So we don't spend much on each other or make a big thing of exchanging gifts. Those things don't mean as much as how we treat each other the rest of the year."

Tad looked around the room. It had no radio, no telephone, no luxuries by the standards of the 1940s. The car out in the shed at the side of the weathered barn was a Model T.

Ben continued. "Sometimes I've ordered Ellie something from a catalog, but she always said I shouldn't have, then complained she could have made it cheaper herself."

Tad asked if he planned to cut a Christmas tree.

"Don't think so," Ben said. "I used to bring in a cedar which we would decorate with strings of popcorn and sycamore balls wrapped in tinfoil. Now I know Christmas is in your head and heart, not in decorations and gifts." He paused a moment, the smile gone from his face. "Oh, if we had kids or grandkids, it might be different."

Tad nodded. "Do you ever wish someone would bring you a gift, just to surprise you on Christmas?"

The smile returned to Ben's face. "I just never think about it. It's better not to expect something. That way you won't be disappointed when you don't get it."

Tad talked for a few more minutes, returned home and told his mom about the conversation.

A few days later he again checked on Ben and Ellie, this time with a bucket in one hand and a bag cradled under his other arm.

Ellie took the bucket and removed the Christmas paper to find homemade candy, cookies, shiny red apples, tangerines and oranges.

"You can open this," Tad told Ben, offering him the sack.

It contained gloves and socks, which needed no darning, for both Ben and Ellie, and a comforter Tad's mom and other women in the neighborhood had made at one of their quilting bees.

Gratefulness moistened the eyes of both Ben and Ellie. Their smiles deepened the furrowed wrinkles in their aging faces.

"Enjoy some cookies," Tad said, "and I'll be right back." He cleared a path through the snow to the barn for Ben, then split a stack of sassafras for Ellie's kitchen range and filled the wood box near the stove.

Both Ben and Ellie thanked him. "Sorry we don't have anything for you," Ellie said.

"Don't worry about it," Tad said, leaving a "Merry Christmas" behind as he walked out the door.

Shocking Experience

Ben had always been independent, able to take care of himself, which may explain why he hemmed and hawed that afternoon. He wasn't about to come right out and ask for help, even though he was old, bent and on the down slope of life.

"Need to cut and shock that patch of corn over there," he said, looking across the road to one of his small fields.

"Always cut some corn," he said. "Wouldn't be the same if I couldn't drag in the shocks on a sled in the winter so I could husk the corn in the barn gangway and feed the fodder to them old cows of mine."

He paused, tried to stand tall, wincing as he placed his hands on his hips. "I just don't feel up to it, though."

Tad's father looked at Ben, then Tad and Tyke. "It's time the boys learned how to cut corn. It's not right for them to get through life without knowing some of its hardships. Let them do it for you."

It was the early 1940s and most farmers around Heltonville had stopped cutting corn years earlier. Tad looked at Tyke, a big "Huh?" written across his face.

Tyke raised his eyes toward the clear blue skies.

"Pay you a quarter a shock," Ben said. "Start whenever you want," he told the two teen-agers before starting for home. The promise to pay was of little consolation. Neither was their father's response to their protests.

"It'll build your character," he said, "and give you some idea of how things used to be done."

He had two corn knives sharpened when they arrived home from school the next day. He walked with Tad and Tyke to Ben's field, showed them how to tie four stalks a yard apart in a square to form a skeleton for a shock. He then took one of the knives, slashed off stalks at 45-degree angles, letting them fall into the cradle he formed with his free arm. Once he had an arm load he laid it at an angle into the frame he had fashioned.

"That'll give you an idea how it is done," he said. "Just keep adding to the shock until you can barely hug it at arm level, then tie it," he added, nodding toward a roll of binder twine.

He left his sons to work. They turned the assignment into a game. Tad posed as a swashbuckler, a sword-wielding adventurer attacking stalks of corn. Tyke was a pioneer, slashing his way forward through an uncharted forest.

They did not take the work seriously. They were more interested in speed than in artistry. The shocks were irregular in shape and size, some listing west, some east; not one stood straight or firm against the winds of the winter to come.

By milking time on that first afternoon, they had cut only an acre. "This will take every afternoon this week," Tad moaned, not seeing his dad approaching.

"It may take longer than that," he screamed. "From now on, I want you to do it right if it takes two weeks. Remember, if you are going to do something, do it right." It was an adage they had heard often.

Ben was more subtle. The next afternoon, he was in the field, trying as best he could to build a shock, sweat flooding the gullies of his face, dampening the bandana around his wrinkled neck.

Tad and Tyke knew he was sending them a message. They worked more slowly, playing the role of farmers, not pirates and pioneers, fashioning a shock that was round and straight, an anchor against the wind.

Ben looked relieved, said nothing, except that he needed to do something back at the barn. He turned so neither Tad nor Tyke could see the conniving smile that crossed his face.

"I think we've been had," Tyke said, without taking his eyes off the row he was cutting. "Yeah," Tad said. "I guess it's never too late for an old dog to teach a young pup."

They finished their work a few days later. Even their dad was pleased. And Ben admitted he couldn't have done a better job himself, "except for that first day."

Tad and Tyke felt so good the money seemed unimportant —until they got a chance to spend it.

A Deeper Meaning

Ben sat under a shade tree in his yard, cooling himself with a Day, Carter & Roach Funeral Home fan snitched from church. He looked at peace with himself, a man with his life nearly complete and satisfied with its outcome.

It was a warm day and Tad had cut through Ben's barn lot, past his house, on his way home after a dip in Back Creek. The swim had cooled him for a time, but the afternoon sun again baked his bare shoulders and dampened his forehead.

Ben returned his greeting.

"Better sit for a spell," Ben said, pulling the pocket watch from the fob in his bib overalls to check the time. "You don't have to be home to milk yet."

He got up slowly, his bones creaking from almost 70 years of use, pumped a cool cup of water and handed it to Tad. It was the early 1940s and farm homes around Heltonville didn't have refrigerators to make ice cubes to drop into soft drinks or lemonade.

Some of Tad's friends thought Ben was cantankerous, grouchy, a difficult man to understand. He was never that way with Tad, who lived across the way on another farm. The two had become comrades; two generations—daybreak and twi-light—bridged by a bond of friendship.

Tad, who was 12, drank the water in a gulp, looked at Ben and asked, more for conversation than information: "Are you and Ellie going to celebrate the Fourth of July?" Tad already knew the answer.

Ben seldom left the farm, regardless of the occasion. If Ellie ever went anywhere, no one knew about it.

Ben shook his head. "Got everything I need to observe the day right here," he said.

"You have fireworks?" Tad asked, grinning so Ben would know he was joshing.

Ben laughed. "No firecrackers, no skyrockets. Just this," he said, waving his arms around the fields and woods that surrounded his home.

"I know," he told Tad, "that the Fourth means you'll see friends you haven't seen since school was out, that you'll be able to get ice cream treats, maybe a hot dog or two, enjoy some carnival rides up at Freetown, watch the big fireworks at Bedford, have a good time from morning 'til well after dark."

Tad nodded.

"That's fine," Ben said. "But I've learned that every day is a time to celebrate freedom. Oh, it's nice, I guess, to have a big shebang once a year to remind us it's Independence Day, to let almost everyone but farmers take the day off. I just don't need to leave home to enjoy myself."

Tad wondered how Ben would spend the holiday.

"Like any other day," Ben said. "I'll do what little chores I have to do, come out here and enjoy myself without being told what to do, except when Ellie gives me an order. I haven't read the Declaration of Independence for a long, long time. But that's freedom to me."

And it doesn't cost anything, Tad thought. "So long," he said, leaving Ben to sit alone by himself and enjoy the company. A man couldn't ask any more than to be both free and content.

End Of An Era

Coated with dust and cobweb blankets, the binder sat undisturbed in the tool shed.

In Junes past, it would have been cleaned, oiled, its working parts checked, broken sections on its cutting bar replaced. A few days after that, it would have cut the ripening wheat, rye and oats, spitting out twine-tied sheaves that would be placed in shocks dotting his small fields until the threshing crew arrived.

Ben had been reluctant to give up the past, to surrender to progress, but he knew it was useless. He had tried to forestall the inevitable; had sought to have the threshing machine return for another year.

He had relented a couple of years back to the progress; had allowed another farmer with a combine to harvest his wheat and rye. He wasn't pleased with the outcome, poking the ground with his cane, pointing out grain the combine had lost. And there was no straw stack near his barn; no bedding for his livestock in the winter to come.

The next year, he had cut his crops with the binder, knowing the crew of men who swapped work would show up when the thresher did. They would help, even though he was too old to make the rounds with them, for he was a neighbor and they were his friends.

He smiled as the steam engine and separator lumbered up the gravel road to his farm east of Heltonville. He had tried to help, as best he could but he was no match for the men and boys who were decades younger.

Ben's farm wasn't big and his entire crop was threshed in that one afternoon. He looked at the wheat the men had scooped into his granary, walked around the straw stack, its stems glistening in the late afternoon sun.

He did not yet know he had seen the end of an era. That was 1941.

Now it was 1942. And the world had changed. The United States was at war; young men who had worn denim shirts and straw hats and worked on the threshing ring were now at Army camps. Help was scarce. Farmers were told to plant fence-row-to-fence-row. The pace of life quickened. Neighbors sought ways to do more in less time with fewer hired hands.

Ben knew, without being told, that no steam engine, no separator, no teams of horses and hay wagons with men propped on three-tined pitchforks would visit his farm later that summer.

"Maybe, once the war is over things will get back to normal," Ben said, more to convince himself than a neighborhood youngster who had stopped to visit.

He was not ready to admit a time that would not return had passed.

* * * * * *

A few weeks later, Doc and Ed harvested Ben's fields with a new Allis Chalmers combine. The dust on the binder grew thicker. It was a relic that would remain on the farm as long as Ben did.

Waste Not, Want Not

Solid waste disposal didn't bother Ben one whit. He seldom threw anything away. When he did he tossed it into a pile for the junk man or dumped it into one of the ditches that had gulleyed the farm he was trying to restore.

Ben farmed from about 1920-1950, back before disposable this and disposable that.

Chicken mash came in cloth sacks that later became dresses and fertilizer in burlap bags that could be used forever.

Tools and machinery weren't complicated. They were made to be repaired, not to be cast aside when broken. Ben had a Model T Ford to take him to town even into the 1940s, but he didn't make the trip often. There was no need. If something broke he fixed it.

He found more uses for baling wire than Watkins salesmen could for the petro-carbo salve they pedaled.

"Fix about anything with baling wire," he told Tad one winter day when the boy rode over for one of his Saturday morning visits.

Tad watched as Ben wired new license plates on the front and back of the Model T.

He held up one of the old plates and said, "Your dad can fix that hole in the muffler of his Chevy with this and some wire. Just bend the plate over the hole and wire it on," he said.

Tad nodded. Ben noticed the boy's overshoes.

"Take that left boot off, boy, and I'll patch that hole," he said. He reached for a container on a shelf, used the raspy top to scuff and clean around the hole in the boot, applied some glue, then attached a rubber patch.

"Good as new," he said, handing the boot back to Tad. "Wanta help me fix the yard gate?" he asked.

Tad nodded. Ben looked at an old set of harness he no longer needed, then cut off two strips of leather with his pocket knife.

Tad looked curious. "You're going to see hinges made from leather?" Ben said.

Tad held the gate in place. Ben attached the leather strips, one end of each to the gate, the other ends to the post. The gate swung back and forth, easily, quietly. "No need to buy metal hinges," Ben decided, latching the gate with links cut from an overlong porch swing chain.

He retrieved his broken spectacles that had fallen on the frozen ground and squinted. "I can fix them with tape," he added, undisturbed, as he returned to the shop, which he called a "car shed."

Ropes, string, chains and wire hung from nails between pliers, metal cutters, saws, hammers, single trees and innertubes. Machinery parts extended from barrels and boxes. Nuts and bolts filled buckets.

"Don't you ever throw anything away?" Tad asked.

Ben didn't mind the impertinence. "Not often. I just find a new use for it," he said.

* * *

Ben's old wire-rimmed glasses would be stained with tears if he could come back 50 years later and see the trash and junk that now line some county roads near his home.

PART IX

Assorted Characters

Other men helped "The Country Bumpkin Gang" on its travel into adolescence, men like Wes, Smith and Harry and Everett, and especially "Doc." And O.G., Luke, and Sharm.

Each was different, each had a distinct personality, each possessed characteristics worth remembering.

Wes, the father, Smith and Harry, the sons, could have been the original organic farmers. They used no fertilizer, knowing the manure they had spread from the barn would darken the corn that grew in bottom land corn fields. They used no hybrids, owned no tractors, drove no cars.

They had money, though. And they loaned it to neighbors at a lower interest than the bank, sometimes taking a man's word rather than his IOU.

O.G. was the "Old Grouch," but his pessimism wasn't contagious.

Luke was an entrepreneur, a man who made the best of what he had to work with. He didn't have much, didn't want a lot more and seemed willing to hand his last dollar to a needier person whom he had just given the shirt off his back.

Everett, unlike Ben, was ahead of his time, living on a farm that looked like it ought to be pictured in "Country Gentleman" magazine. Sharm, like Ben, was slow to change, but he was more outgoing, able to ignore the indiscretions of youth, turn enemies into friends.

"Doc" Cain brought babies into the world, cured the sick and found happiness in all things great and small.

Taylor, on occasions, proved that he could get up and go. He just didn't like to get up and go too often. And Bart, as a farmer, talked a better game than he played, but he, also, had redeeming qualities.

The "Bumpkins" were better off for having known each of them.

Wes, Smith, Harry

A bag of hybrid seed corn looked like a bag of seed corn to Tad, the grains in the sack the same as from ears in the crib.

He wouldn't have given the "Pioneer—Variety 312" lettering on the sack much thought as he helped his dad plant corn that spring morning had it not been for an earlier visit to Wes's farm down in the Back Creek bottoms.

Wes and his boys, Harry and Smith, walked a different furrow, hoed a different row than most farmers.

It was the early 1940s and they still used horses to pull the breaking plows, tow the disks and cultipackers and power the corn planters through their fields. And they still used seed corn shelled from ordinary ears in the crib long after hybrids, like Pioneer, were developed.

Actually Harry and Smith weren't boys, Wes just called them that. They were middle-aged, had grown up on the farm, doing things the way their dad had done, letting others buy tractors, labor-saving equipment . . . and hybrid seed corn.

Wes had shaken his head when Tad's father asked him if he intended to plant hybrid that season. He would stick with his own seed, he said. "Always get a good crop, don't see any reason to change," he said.

Tad knew better than to get involved in adult conversations. He had read a story in an encyclopedia at school about how hybrid seed was developed. Corn breeders at universities had cross pollinated two varieties to get an even better one.

For example, one variety might resist disease better than another. A second strain might produce larger ears than the first. They were then crossbred, the male tassels in selected rows dropping onto the female silk on stalks in detasseled rows, thus producing a hybrid. This meant farmers had to buy seed if they wanted to plant a hybrid.

Tad remembered that as he and his dad walked up the hollow toward home, their eyes darting among the wildflowers, hoping to spot a late mushroom.

"Wonder why Wes doesn't plant hybrid?" he asked.

"Don't know," his dad said. "But a lot of farmers didn't at first." He related some of the arguments he had heard farmers make when hybrid became available back in the 1930s.

"I remember Clem sayin' that if God wanted animals and plants to crossbreed he wouldn't have made them the way they are." And Hiram complained, 'If there had been crossbreeds in Noah's time, his ark would have had to be three miles long to get everything on board.' And Hecky said he wasn't about to crossbreed a Chester White boar with a Poland China sow to see what he got."

Tad laughed.

"Some people," his dad said, "used to think crossbreeding was evil. I read somewhere that the word hybrid once meant insult or outrage. I guess that's why some people had to be shown that hybrid corn was an exception to that definition. It just takes time for people to change," he added, "and sometimes it's not good when they do."

He leaned over, removed his old felt hat and filled it with big yellow morels.

"You think Wes will ever switch to hybrid seed?" Tad asked.

"Someone will come up with a hybrid morel mushroom first," his dad answered.

Tad knew that would never happen. Morel mushrooms were among those things too good to change.

So were Wes, Smith and Harry. They were good, sturdy, dependable; rocks among pebbles, oaks among saplings.

Unlike fields of corn, tampering would not have made them better.

An Old Grouch

Chances are O.G. awoke each morning wondering how to turn a silver lining into a dark cloud.

O.G. wasn't his real name. Other farmers sometimes around Heltonville called him Old Grouch, more in jest than in the spirit of meanness. It was their sons who shortened Old Grouch into O.G.

O.G. wasn't a bad sort. He just couldn't see the sun for the umbrella of gloom he carried over his frail body.

He seemed old to boys of 12, who thought 45 was ancient. He would have looked younger, but he seldom shaved for fear he'd cut himself with the straight razor, and didn't always wear his false teeth, lest they break. He figured if anything could go wrong it would happen to him.

The Great Depression had ended, but O.G. still didn't trust banks, seldom bought anything lest he get "skinned," as he called it. He didn't own a dog, for fear that it might run out on the gravel road and be hit by one of the four or five cars that passed by each day.

His neighbors wondered why he bothered to plant corn, sow wheat, there being only a 99.8 percent chance the seeds would grow. They sought to bring O.G. into the brotherhood of optimists, attempted to brighten his day with humor; even tried to goad him through taunts in an effort to improve his disposition.

Oh, he might cheer up for a time, but he never gave joy more than a short-term lease on his thoughts. He swapped work with his neighbors, followed the threshing ring from farm to farm and was no slacker when hard labor was concerned.

Threshing crews gave him an audience for his disillusionment, but, try as he would, he couldn't dim the zest other farmers had for the camaraderie of the harvest.

It was Zeke who tried hardest to change O.G., to turn him from pessimist to optimist. "Enjoy the good days," he said, "for they always outnumber the bad. And if something does go bad, all of us are here to help," he added, waving his hand around the shade tree where the men rested after dinner.

O.G. looked at him and replied, "Chances are, the undertaker will have to get me out of the casket to dig my own grave," he said. The other men laughed. O.G. didn't.

A few years passed, the seasons changed, but O.G. stayed the same, then became ill. Perhaps his mind had convinced his body that it, too, was susceptible to harm. It was harvest time and combines had replaced the binder and the threshing machine. O.G. was certain his small acreage of wheat would rot in the field.

He needn't have worried. Zeke drove his combine down the road, another farmer followed with his truck, and soon O.G.'s crop was sold at the grain elevator. A smile crossed his face when he saw the check. It grew even wider when Zeke and the other men turned down any pay.

O.G. died a few years after that . . . and all his neighbors showed up to dig his grave.

Farmer's Guide

Everett was as old as yesterday, as new as today, unafraid of tomorrow. As a farmer, he was ahead of his time, open to progress, eager to move forward with the march of time.

He was in the autumn of life, around 65, when Tad began to notice his farm in the early 1940s. His barn, the "Everett Foster" name labeled on the front, was newly painted. So were the outbuildings. The grounds around the white house were manicured, fences straight. Nothing was out of place.

It was a show place compared to most farms in Eastern Lawrence County, where implements sometimes remained outdoors, buildings went unpainted and fences tilted on decaying locust posts.

No ditches cut through Everett's fields, no bulrushes cluttered his fence rows or property lines. He was a steward of the land, a conservationist before it was popular to be one.

Everett lived south of Heltonville in a different township and he seldom came into town to shop. He was more likely to drive to

Bedford, maybe to confer with the county agricultural agent, or attend, as a director, a meeting of the Dunn Memorial Hospital Board.

That's why Tad seldom saw him, didn't know him other than by sight, was more in awe of him than he was farmers who lived further to the east and closer to his home.

Oh, he waved at Everett when he passed his place on Powerline Road, or Clearspring Road, as some people called it. But he learned, by listening to his dad, about Everett the man and Everett the farmer.

Everett was a song leader and Sunday School teacher at the Erie Methodist Church not far from his home. He sang with a church quartet, even gave voice lessons, which seemed strange to Tad who knew most farmers couldn't carry a tune in a syrup bucket. Everett, though, was genteel in a time of rugged individualists.

He was a charter member of the county Farm Bureau Co-op, a Farm Bureau director, a man who had for 25 years found time to keep records of his income and expenses for the Purdue University farm management department.

Other farmers had come to him for advice, especially after "Prairie Farmer" magazine named him its master farmer of 1936.

Tad, knowing all that, was a bit apprehensive the first time he talked with Everett. Everett was well-known, a man with a lifetime of accomplishments. Tad was a high school youngster, an unsure teen-ager, without merit badges. He need not have worried.

Everett treated him as an equal, was in no rush to cut off the conversation, asked more questions than he answered, suggested they talk again soon.

Tad's father wasn't surprised when he related his experience, explaining: "Everett's like that. The higher a man goes in life, the more likely he is to reach down and help those on the way up."

Everett Foster died 15 or so years later. The obituary writer at the Bedford Times-Mail called him "a retired farmer." He was that . . . and a lot more.

Cross Ties

It was Tad's good fortune to be at Roberts General Store in Heltonville that day in the late 1930s.

He was no more than ten, seldom had a nickel for either a soft drink or a candy bar, the Great Depression having left pockets empty and coffers bare. Which is why Tad was surprised when Luke, sporting a week's growth of whiskers, said, "Pop for everybody. On me."

Bob Roberts, one of the store operators, counted heads. "Eleven drinks, 55 cents."

Tad stood in line behind the men, waited his turn at the cooler, removed a Royal Crown Cola and eased the cap from the bottle. He didn't know Luke well, but he copied the motions of the other men, raising his drink in thanks for the treat.

"You find a gold mine back in them hills?" someone asked Luke.

"Might say that," Luke replied. He was a big man, muscles on muscles so hard he appeared to have arms of iron. His hands were as big as the mitt the catcher for the Heltonville Merchants wore.

Most men had grown soft over a long winter that on most days had kept farmers from outdoor work and timbermen out of the woods. It was obvious Luke hadn't missed many hours of hard labor.

"Tell us about your good fortune," Hobe said, eying Luke curiously.

Luke finished his Coke, fished another bottle from the cooler tank, laid down a buffalo nickel on the cash register and went into a monologue. "I don't believe in them WPA jobs. They're just government make-work that cost taxpayers," he said.

"That's why I've spent the last few years hewing cross ties. Cut them for a middle man on his place for 10 cents a tie, which brought me about a $1 a day. I busted myself one day and cut 13. My boss hemmed and hawed and said, 'Ain't no one worth $1.30 a day.' Guess he didn't realize them 'We Piddle Around' workers get $2."

Tad knew "We Piddle Around" was what many folks around town called the WPA. He also had watched men hew cross ties, knew it was about the hardest labor a man could do, swinging a broad axe hour after hour, turning logs into eight-by-eight-inch square timbers eight feet long.

Luke sipped the last of his second Coke. "That's when I got smart. I figured I could cut trees on my own place, hew the ties and sell them direct to a buyer for a quarter each.

"Just brought in another wagon load of 20 ties," he said, jingling some change in his overall pocket. "That's my team and wagon out there."

"So they brought $5," someone figured.

"Nope. $4.80," Luke said. "Got a quarter for all but one. It was a 'cull' and brought only a nickel. Which one of you is drinking the cull?" he laughed.

Everyone knew a cull was a tie that was substandard.

Luke went on. "Now if I could just sell them direct to the Milwaukee Railroad, I might get 35 cents each for 'em."

He thought for a second, then added, "No matter! I'm making a lot more money now that I'm in business for myself."

Tad looked at the clock. He had a five-mile hike home and milking to do when he got there. He walked toward the door, turned and said, "Thanks, Luke." Some of the others repeated their appreciation for his treat.

A grin spread across Luke's face. "Easy come, easy go. Think nothin' of it."

Old-Fashioned Goodness

Sharm owned a car, but he seldom drove it. Never felt at ease in "the confounded thing," as he called his puddle jumper.

He'd had plenty of time to become adjusted to it, having had it for 15 years. But he still preferred to live in 1940 like he did in 1910. Oh, he might drive the car once in a while in the summer, never in winter. He could always find a ride to the county seat with a neighbor if he needed to go, which was only in the fall and spring to pay his real estate taxes.

The rest of the time he would drive to Heltonville or Norman in his horse-drawn wagon with steel-rimmed wheels, ignoring the cars that sped around him.

He could accomplish a lot in one trip; have livestock feed ground, wheat turned into flour at the elevator, swap chickens for groceries at the general store, maybe ask the clerk to scoop chocolates into a sack he could nibble on en route home.

He didn't run a bill like a lot of folks did. If he couldn't pay for or swap for whatever he needed, he didn't buy it. Credit was something men in town ran.

Zeke, Clem and other farmers accepted him for being independent, if a bit eccentric. It was teen-agers from town who judged him from his appearance and actions, knowing not the depth of his character, or the contentment his familiarity with the past gave him.

Sometimes they were rude, easing up behind his wagon, then blasting the horns of the cars they drove, trying to frighten his team. Sometimes they laughed as they passed, slowing down to shout comments he had heard before. He paid them no heed, for he knew that eventually the world might catch and pass them as it had him.

It was good that Sharm did not carry a grudge, especially for "Slim" and "Rusty." The two young "whipper snappers," as some people called them, knocked at his door one night, waited for Sharm to light a coal oil lamp and come to the door, then confessed, sheepishly, "We need your help."

Sharm nodded himself awake, having been asleep in his feather bed.

"My car's hung up in a side ditch," one of them said. "Wonder if you might help us get it out?"

Sharm, too kind to do otherwise, didn't ask where they had been. "The thaw has made the roads go through," he explained. "Go through" was a term used to explain when the mud eased up through the gravel and the gravel disappeared into the mud.

"Can't be much help at my age," he admitted. "I don't have a tractor. Could pull you out, maybe, with the team unless you still think horse power is 'old-fashioned and outdated.' "

Rusty's face grew red in the dim lamp light. He had caught the barbs Sharm had used to prick his conscience. "We'd appreciate it," he said.

Rusty and Slim followed as Sharm led the way to the barn, lantern in hand. He harnessed his horses, hitched them to a double tree he took from the wagon, wrapped a thick rope around his arm, and said, "Lead the way."

The car was mired to its axle, the edges of the road a quagmire. "Looks pretty bad," Sharm said.

He tied the rope to the bumper. "One of you push, the other steer," he said, his one-time detractors obedient. He clucked his tongue, a signal for the horses to move. They strained against the harness, bringing the rope taut as their hooves sank into the mud.

Slowly they plodded forward, the car following. A hundred feet or so ahead the road bed was firm. Sharm stopped, unhooked the team and said, "You should make it okay from here."

A month or two later, Sharm returned to town riding high in the seat on his wagon bed. None of the teens sitting on the bread box in front of the store laughed. Slim and Rusty saw to that. They waved.

Sharm returned their salute.

Break Time

A boy could learn a lot about men by working with them on farms back in the early 1940s.

Some men were teachers, who shared what they had learned through experience. Some were quiet role models to be watched rather than heard. Still others were talkers whose words often exceeded their wisdom.

"Doc" Cain was a teacher. He had closed his doctor's office in Heltonville, leaving the shelter from the weather for the freedom of the outdoors.

It gave him time to share his thoughts, his experiences, on sweltering summer days during wheat harvest. He explained how to tie a miller's knot; how to bandage a young rabbit's leg that had been severed by a combine, how to determine the bushels in a truck bed by its dimensions.

His time, it seemed, belonged to the young. Maybe it was because he had brought them into the world; perhaps owed them some responsibility. He taught them happiness did not come from money, wealth or position, but from within.

Zeke taught by example. He was quiet as are many men of character; didn't explain in detail how work was to be done. He was to be watched, for he could do almost any chore on a farm better, more quickly, than anyone in the neighborhood.

Teens learned from him how to shock wheat. Or stick a hay fork into a wagon of loose hay, then dump it as it ran across a track at the top of the barn; how to plant, cultivate, harvest; how to tend to animals and care for machinery.

They observed him as he worked, watched his fluid, unwasted motions as he used a scythe, a crosscut saw or a double-edge axe.

Bart was unlike either "Doc" or Zeke. He was a self-styled expert on any facet of farm life, had answers to the world's problems, offered suggestions about how to rid the Pacific of Japanese and Europe of its German captors.

Teens, though, soon learned that Bart talked a better game than he played. His crops weren't as good as Zeke's; his thoughts more shallow than "Doc's."

A dollar was a dollar, though, and Tad and Bugsy always agreed to help when Bart called. That's how they happened to be in the hayfield with him one hot sticky summer day. Bugsy was stacking the loose clover on the wagon. Tad was throwing shocks up to him, when Bart called a time out.

He wanted the stage for one of his lectures. "The art of pitching hay," it could have been called. "You are too jerky with your motions," he told Tad. "Watch me and you'll see how I raise the hay in a smooth motion."

He demonstrated what he meant with his arms, minus the pitchfork and the hay. Tad nodded, having been taught to respect his elders. He watched as Bart followed the hay wagon to the next shock.

"Now pay attention," Bart glowered. He jabbed the three-tined fork into the shock and started to lift it. The handle of the fork split, jaggedly, the hay falling limply onto the stubbled field. Bart was left holding half of a splintered handle.

His face turned red as the bandana around his neck. "They don't make pitchforks like they used to," he snarled. He headed for the barn to get another.

Tad resumed loading the clover, ignoring Bart's coaching, going through the same motions he had always used.

"Betcha you don't get any more lectures today," Bugsy said.

He was right. Bart, for the rest of the afternoon, was as speechless as a sphinx.

A Cure-All

Health care wasn't a big issue in the Heltonville area around 1940. "Doc" Cain saw to that.

"Doc's" real name was Jasper, but few people called him that. About the only time he let patients use his given name was when they wrote checks to pay a bill.

That didn't happen too often, though, especially in those long depression years of the 1930s.

"Doc" had two loves, people and the Southern Indiana hills and fields where they lived. He had spent decades making house calls on horseback, at times, later by car, delivering babies, treating the sick, leaving medication, making everyone in a household feel better whether they were ill or not.

He would arrive on spring days, several feet behind his shadow, a black bag in his right hand, a cigar in his left and a smile on his face.

He would close a door behind, the bedroom becoming an examining room or a maternity room.

"Doc" seldom seemed to be in a hurry, never rushed off as soon as he'd brought a bawling baby into the world or ordered a quarantine for measles. He had time for coffee and conversation, which sometimes substituted for cash.

He knew most families would eventually pay him, even if it was in eggs and butter instead of cash. Money didn't concern him much, now that he had a farm out on Henderson Creek, a nice home in Heltonville and a little office next door to the post office.

It wasn't necessary to call "Doc" for an appointment. A patient could walk in, take a seat and wait a few minutes for him to step from a back room.

"Doc" seemed to know everyone. Those he didn't he'd ask their name, then say, "Oh, you're Pete's boy" or "That's right, Joe and Elvira's daughter."

He was more than a country doctor, though. He served a couple of terms as Pleasant Run Township trustee, administering the school system, hiring principals and teachers, handling the payroll. A man, he reasoned, ought to do more for his community than use it to make a living or amass a fortune.

That probably explains why he gave up his practice in the early 1940s. By then, almost every family had an automobile. A hospital, and other doctors, were just 15 minutes or so away in Bedford so he was not leaving them without medical care.

It was time for "Doc" to spend his days on the land, making it better as he had its people. He helped his son, Ed, farm the bottom land, then joined him as they took their Allis Chalmers tractor and combine around the area harvesting grain for farmers.

That gave "Doc" more time to spend with Tad and Tyke and other boys he'd seen enter the world and begin the journey into manhood. He shared his wisdom, listened to their concerns, offered advice from the reservoir of his own life. When the combine sliced a leg from a spring rabbit, he shredded his big handkerchief to fashion a tourniquet and form a bandage for life, in any form, was important to him.

He never forgot he was a doctor and his black bag was never far away.

Not even wildlife had to fret about health care when "Doc" was around.

Not Habit Forming

Taylor didn't have much of what farmers called "get up and go." He had no regular job and, as far as anyone knew, didn't care whether he had one or not. Money, or the lack of it, didn't seem to bother him much.

Taylor lived with his family in a little frame house back in the woods off Ind. 58 between Heltonville and Norman. He didn't have a car, which was just as well, because he didn't have a lot of desire to go anywhere.

He could walk, maybe hitch a ride, when he needed to go into town to pick up a few staples.

His wife did her own hair, Taylor's too, using a pair of ordinary scissors already dulled from mending their sons' overalls until they were too threadbare to hold a patch.

Life was meant, it seemed to Taylor, to be lived with as little effort as possible. Had there been a contest for inactivity, he would have won.

Which was why Zeke was surprised one June day in the early 1940s when he asked Taylor if he'd like a few days work. The first cutting of red clover was in the field and Zeke was desperate for help, which explains why he asked Taylor despite his reputation as a sluggard.

Most of the able-bodied men Zeke had depended on in earlier years were off fighting the Japanese and Nazis.

Zeke had barely finished his job offer when Taylor broke in. "Be happy to help," he said, not even asking how much he'd be paid.

A couple of other men Zeke had found to help laughed when they learned they'd be working with Taylor. "Don't know whether I can walk slowly enough to stay with him," one of them joked. "I heard you have to put up stakes to make sure he's mo-bile," he said, making mobile two words.

The men were surprised when they arrived at Zeke's place. Taylor already was there, sitting on the flatbed truck, waiting.

One of them said, "I'll stack the bales." "I'll drive," yelled the other, quickly, lest someone else asked for the snap job. Zeke looked at Taylor. "Guess you and I'll have to pick up the bales and toss them on the truck," he said, expecting to do most of the work himself.

He was wrong. Taylor wasn't the slacker he made himself out to be. He ran between bales, tossing them onto the truck, even motioning at times for the truck driver to accelerate as he drove across the stubble.

If Zeke hadn't been lean and wiry, he wouldn't have been able to keep up with Taylor's pace. Taylor had endurance, too. He worked as hard stacking bales in the loft as he did in the field.

And he was moving as fast at 4 p.m. as he had at 11 a.m., as quickly on Thursday as he had on Wednesday, even turning down an offer to drive the truck the last day.

When the work was done, Zeke looked Taylor in the eye and admitted, "You're the best hand I've had in a coon's age. Wish I could afford to hire you full time."

Taylor stuck the pay check Zeke had written into a thin, shapeless wallet and said, "I don't know whether I'd like that or not. Once in a while money does have a way of motivating me." A big grin crossed his face as he added, "But I don't like to be motivated too often."

PART X

Barber Shop Banter

Bugsy, Chig and the gang never forgot the incidents they observed and the stories they heard at barber shops. They banked them in their memory vaults, and drew upon them for interest in years to come.

Barber shops were more for fun than for grooming. Men gathered to swap stories, more true than false, real life at the time being more exciting than fiction.

It was a time when men, their whiskers a week old, were shaved by barbers, who honed straight razors on a whetstone and stropped them on a strip of leather. Hardened men mumbled, through hot towels, that they were being scalded as their beards were being softened.

Boys, for the most part learned to keep quiet, being no match for men who had spent decades telling stories, learning to spice their conversations with descriptive words.

Bees In Bras

Men still swap stories, but not the way they did a half-century ago. The color has faded from conversations.

Story tellers now sound like TV commentators. They watch their grammar, punctuate their phrases and choose their words like they were in Dale Carnegie speech classes.

The result is language that's deader than a door nail, flatter than a fritter, as dull as dishwater.

Reckon that's to be expected from highfalutin, would-be muckety-mucks who are interested in puttin' on the dog and makin' folks think the sun rises to hear them crow.

Harken back a half-century to a time when farmers around Heltonville spiced their language with realism, not rhetoric, when they met at barber shops. They stole phrases from others, coined their own and mixed them into sentences that told stories as descriptive and colorful as pictures of the autumn landscape.

The didn't just feel well or poorly. They felt tolerably well, downright puny, had no gumption or get-up-and-go and would have to get better to die.

If they showed up at the barber shop down-in-the-mouth, the ol' razor stropper told them they looked like they'd been rode hard and put away wet.

No one entered the shop to get his ears set out without a customer telling the others, "Look at what the cat drug in." Anyone who protested was told not to have a conniption.

The men had their own view of the opposite sex. Some women were as purty as pictures, as cute as ponies in pig lots, as sweet as maple sugar.

Some, the men, said, had faces that could stop newly-wound seven-day clocks. Some were as ugly as mud fences. Some were as homely as lye soap.

If a less-than-pretty woman walked by, someone would observe, "She can't help it if she's ugly, but she could stay home."

A man with muscles like rocks would be stronger than an ox, could go bear hunting with a switch or scare the bejabbers out of a stranger.

Youngsters who were doing cartwheels and somersaults on the grass across the road flopped around like chickens with their heads cut off.

Some baseball or basketball players were faster than greased lightning. Others were as sluggish as sorghum in January, as slow as February, or so pokey bread crumbs wouldn't fall off when they walked. A few were as awkward as pregnant sows on ice.

Some boys were as sharp as tacks, a few had minds as quick as steel traps, some had brains but no horse sense.

Not all kids were smart. Some were as green as gourds. If some had a brain it would die of loneliness. Boys who were naive looked like they'd just fallen off a hay wagon on the road to nowhere.

A complete ne'er-do-well wasn't worth the salt that went into his bread. A scoundrel wasn't worth the powder it'd take to blow him off a rail fence.

Now and then a farmer would complain he was too poor to pay attention, let alone his taxes. The truth was, almost all of them were actually happier than hogs in slop.

Some of the men lived high on the hog, but others had to eat one day and swallow the next.

None of the men spent too much time in the barber shop, or anywhere else, lest they plant their feet in concrete or get set in their ways. Besides, they were all busier than bees in bras or one-armed paper hangers at fall house cleaning. There was so much work to do they didn't even have time to cuss the cat.

They needed time to be alone. After all, it took a heap of thinkin' to conjure up new sayin's that would bring tears to a glass eye.

A Dog's Day

Loafers in the barber shop at Heltonville had about run out of topics to debate when Slim walked in.

It was a Saturday morning, cold like most early February days, and the men had already discussed the weather, the Friday night basketball game, the war, the timber business and hog prices.

Slim was an outdoorsman, liked to hunt, and could give as well as take in the friendly war of words the men often waged in the early 1940s. A seven-day stubble of graying whiskers covered his wind-whipped face.

Small icicles, formed from moisture, dangled on his forehead from the sock cap he wore. "Did the milkin' in the warm barn, then the chores out in the cold," he said, looking at Tad who had eyed the icicles, curiously.

Slim was still unbuttoning his fleece-lined denim coat when Clem asked:

"How's them ol' coon dogs of your'n adoin'?"

Tad knew "your'n dogs adoin'" meant "how are your dogs doing?"

Slim was a raccoon hunter. So were some of the other men. Those who weren't had dogs they loved almost as much as their wives and kids. Dogs named Shep, Rover, Monster; never sissy names like Fido or Fluffy.

Slim looked at Clem. "You'd think even a blind dog could find a bone now and then. Not General. He's always barking up the wrong tree." General was one of his dogs.

"If my boys didn't like him so much, I'd get rid of him in two shakes of a dog's hind leg." It was obvious Slim wasn't going to be serious about his coon hunting experiences of the past week. The joy was the sport itself, not bragging about it later.

"Sounds to me like you got a dog that won't hunt," Zeke said.

The other men joined in the exchange.

"You ought to give General another chance," Clarence said. "Coon eyes don't shine down on the same dog every day."

Pete suggested he retire General. "After all he's led a dog's life for years."

"Yeah! Make a lap dog outta him," said another man.

Slim was smiling. He'd taken the minds of the men off serious matters. "If I made him a house dog, he'd be too lazy to scratch fleas."

"And be all bark and no bite," added Zeke.

Slim was laughing. "If I'd let him in the kitchen, the old woman would move me out to the dog house."

"Next" Lester the barber called. Slim climbed into the chair, rubbing his beard. "Shave," he ordered.

Someone said, "Better give him a haircut, too. If his mane gets any longer his wife won't be able to tell him from his dogs."

Lester plastered Slim's face with a hot towel before he could respond.

It was time to change the conversation. Laughter might cause Lester's razor to slip when Slim bobbed his Adam's apple.

Slim eased himself out the chair, his face clean, his hair neatly sheared. He buttoned his coat, pulled the sock cap, still damp from the melted ice, over his ears.

"After an hour here, I'm dogged tired," he said, walking out the door.

Zeke shouted after him: "Be careful who you do business with. There are scoundrels out there who are as crooked as a dog's hind leg."

No one said much for a few minutes after the laughter died down.

"You have anything to read?" Tad asked Lester, during the lull in conversation.

Lester nodded toward a corner of the shop. "There's a Collier's over there. But all the pages are dog-eared."

Stranger Within

He was a stranger, but he fit right in with the crowd at the barber shop in Heltonville that icy Saturday morning in January in the early 1940s.

He was from up in Monroe County, Tad thought he heard him say. If he had a reason for being in town, he didn't mention what it was.

No matter! He listened for a while at some of the tall stories the farmers and timbermen wove, then decided he could compete with them.

He gave some background about himself. "I'm a coon hunter," he said. That made him nothing special to the men because they hunted raccoons, too.

His audience razzed him when he added he had a friend named Sam who had the best dog a man could have. "Yeah!, we've all heard about smart dogs," Clem said. "Some of us have dogs we sometimes think are smarter than our wives."

Zeke couldn't let the comment pass. "In your case, Clem, that might be true," he joked.

Clem acted like his feelings were hurt after he managed to stop laughing.

The stranger said he was glad to be among friends, then added, "Let me tell you about my friend Sam's dog."

Zeke laughed. "I think you're going to whether we let you or not."

"Tough crowd," the outsider said, undeterred. "Sam has a friend like you fellers. His name is Kike and he was skeptical, like you men are about Sam's dog. Kike claimed his hound was a lot smarter than Sam's, even proposed that they run the animals through a test so he could prove it."

No one interrupted. The man continued. "Sam asked Kike what kind of test he had in mind, so he suggested they take the dogs down to the creek. Seemed like a funny place for a dog contest, but ol' Sam agreed.

"When he got to the creek, Kike pulled out a quarter, tossed it in the water, which must have been about three feet deep, and told his dog to go fetch the 25-cent piece."

The other men waited in suspense.

The stranger continued. "Kike's dog waded into the water, began to swim, made a dive and came out with the quarter between his teeth. Kike thought he had Sam, claiming the retrieval proved his dog was smarter than his."

A man slid down from the chair. "Next," called the barber, who also was caught up in the story.

The man was on a roll. "Sam told Kike to wait a minute, that his dog hadn't been given a chance to see if he could bring back a quarter. So Kike took the quarter and threw it into the creek again.

"That's when Sam told his dog to show its stuff. That dog went into the water and threshed around maybe 2 or 3 minutes, like maybe he was takin' a bath."

He paused for effect. "Then he came out with a fish about eight inches long in his mouth. You should have heard Kike roar with laughter until Sam took the fish, pulled out his long-bladed pocket knife and sliced open that sucker . . . and exposed the quarter it had swallowed.

"Ol' Kike about croaked. He had to admit Sam's dog was smarter than his."

The barber shook his head. "Dangdest fish story I've ever heard," he concluded. His customers agreed the tale was a whopper that would be difficult to top.

The man left after a few minutes, without a hair cut. He didn't say where he was headed, but the men suspected it was to another barber shop where he could tell the story again.

"She's Still Dead"

Political candidates, in those days before television, held political rallies in church basements throughout southern Indiana. This is a story about one of those events in the early 1940s, revealed at the barber shop.

"Bill, who told me the story, swears it really happened," one of the men said, then proceeded to repeat the tale:

Bill was a township coordinator for a congressman who was seeking re-election, a politician with a glad hand, a friendly back slap and a loose tongue.

Bill had done his job well. He had posted notices about the rally on corner fence posts of every farm in the neighborhood and at general stores within a 10-mile radius. He had urged voters to meet the congressman.

"To know him is to vote for him," he told them. Bill persuaded his wife to bake cookies, "at least 200," he told her. "And get enough coffee for a hundred or so cups," he added. While she baked he lined the church basement with red, white and blue crepe paper, placed the benches in rows and unfolded as many chairs as room allowed.

Bill and his "old lady," as he called her, arrived at the church an hour early, eager for their night in the spotlight. He smelled the coffee brewing and gave his wife a thumbs up as she spread the cookies on a flat tin a yard square. They waited, hoping, apprehensively, that the congressman, who had hobnobbed with dignitaries on Capitol Hill and visited with President Roosevelt, would approve of the less than elegant atmosphere.

Slowly the crowd gathered, hanging coats in a corner and talking about the corn harvest and grain prices after being greeted by Bill. By the time the congressman arrived, the seats were filled and men stood in corners and alcoves.

Bill made the introduction, as formal as his rural roots would permit, and sat down to listen. When the congressman finished he had made the Biblical Promised Land seem secondary to what he had in mind for the area. The crowd, led by Bill, applauded.

It was time for the candidate to work the crowd. Men and women sat down their coffee and cookies, shook his hand and listened as he made them feel he was one of them. He stopped to greet a farmer who tottered on a cane. "How's your wife?" he asked.

The old man, sadness in his eyes, replied softly, "She died six months ago."

The congressman expressed his condolence and moved on.

The old man had shuffled to the cookie table by the time the lawmaker worked through the crowd. Oblivious to faces, he again shook the widower's hand and asked once more, "How's the missus?"

Dropping his hand, the old man frowned. "She's still dead."

The congressman, deaf to his constituents, replied, "That's good," and went on his way.

Election day came and the old man needed a ride to the precinct. Bill didn't offer to take him, knowing it would be one vote the congressman wouldn't get.

PART XI

Women Of Their Lives

"Country Bumpkins" had a special bond with their fathers. They turned to their mothers when things didn't go right.

Fathers taught them how to mend fence, plow, plant, harvest, cut wood and care for the land and the things that live on it. Mothers showed them how to pick berries, make a garden, separate cream from milk, dress neatly, be humble, and care about people as well as things.

Boys sought approval from their fathers, love from their mothers. Fathers were their friends, advisers, confidants. Mothers were their disciplinarians, making them walk the line when their fathers were too permissive.

Fathers taught sons the work ethic, the belief that success belonged to those who earned it. Mothers taught them that work was important and success admirable, but that there also was more to life.

Fathers bought them bib overalls, high-top boots and pocket knives. Mothers saw to it they had dress pants, Sunday shoes, and pocket combs.

Fathers were sometimes caustic, sometimes scathing. Mothers were, it seemed, always even-tempered.

Fathers accepted the fact their sons sometimes wanted to skip church on Sunday mornings. Mothers fretted about their salvation.

Boys bragged to other boys about their fathers. Mothers were taken for granted. But they never complained.

Better Than Butter

Maudie knew a crisis when she faced one, having raised seven kids in a farm house that had no electricity or indoor plumbing.

"Nothing," she complained, "has ever been as bad as this." "This" was the plight she faced that July Saturday in the early 1940s. The preacher and his wife were coming for Sunday dinner the next day and she was certain she would be embarrassed.

Most housewives around Heltonville spared no effort to prepare a meal that would earn the minister's praise. Maudie was no exception.

If home cooked food would get her to heaven, she wanted to earn first class passage. The pastor had never failed to praise Maudie for her biscuits, which he loaded with butter she had churned.

She always beamed when he said, after almost every visit, "Your chicken is great, Maudie, but your biscuits and butter are beyond description." He accented beyond to "beeee . . . . yooonnnd."

Now, she was in distress. The cows, looking for green vegetation in the drought-dried pasture, had digested ragweed, making the milk and the cream from it too distasteful to use.

Setting a table without butter, she thought, would be like a meal without a blessing.

"We do have Oleo," one of her daughters reminded her. Oleo at the time was white and looked more like lard than butter. It came with a package of coloring, which, when mixed, turned the Oleo a pale yellow.

Maudie watched as the Oleo was mixed, then placed in a butter mold for effect. "He will know the difference. He will know the difference," she repeated, giving "he" a reverence it did not merit. "We'll be lucky if he and the missus ever come to dinner again."

Chances are the thought kept her awake that night. She arose early the next morning, fixed the dough for biscuits, happy she had saved enough of the milk that had been separated before the cows consumed the ragweed.

At church, her mind was on dinner, even when the minister sermonized. At the dinner table, the minister prayed so long Maudie thought he might not be hungry.

But she was wrong. He filled his plate with chicken and mash potatoes, peas and green beans fresh from the garden and selected a biscuit from the bread basket. He took pains to pave each half of the biscuit with a quarter inch of the disguised Oleo, then topped it with apple butter. He did the same after a second helping of chicken and vegetables.

Maudie looked on, too curious to do more than tease her food with a fork.

"I'd like another biscuit," the preacher said, taking two to avoid another request. He spread the Oleo once more, this time dividing the halves on the plate, then covering them with maple syrup made from the sap of sugar trees across the road. Maudie was slicing a warm apple pie when the preacher looked up and said, "You know, Maudie, I've eaten at about every house in these parts, but nobody has better tasting biscuits and butter than you."

Maudie thanked him, hoping her face hadn't turned red, ignoring a slight nudge from her conscience to tell him the truth. That night she thanked God for Oleo and asked Him to forgive her for her deceit.

Snake In The Spring

It wasn't like Edie to convict culprits without evidence but she was sure two suspects were guilty.

It had to be her two grandsons—who were spending the summer on the farm — and no one else, she reasoned, who were snitching the cream from the crock in the basin of the spring. For days she had noticed the thin metal lid had been pushed aside, not flush with the top as she had left it. And the cream was an inch or so below the level it had been.

Edie lived on a farm near Heltonville in the 1940s. The spring was under a small milk house where the cream was separated from whole milk in a hand cranked machine appropriately called a separator. She kept the cream for household use in the crock; the cream the produce man would pick up for delivery to a Seymour dairy in a heavier can.

The skim milk that wasn't saved to drink was poured into the hog troughs.

The can was never disturbed, probably because the two grand kids couldn't remove the top, she thought. She had pre-judged Butch and Rusty without a fair trial, so sure she was of their duplicity.

Each day she warned them that if the thievery continued they would soon be eating dry Wheaties or Post Toasties for breakfast. After all the cream in the crock was to be used to churn butter as well as cover cereal and fresh strawberries once they ripened.

It did no good for them to protest their innocence, no point in telling her that they had no taste for cream. Their stomachs were filled with the warm skimmed milk they caught in tin cups as it came from the separator spout each morning and night.

It was a week or so later when Edie learned she had wrongly accused Butch and Rusty. She had just started down the steps to the spring when she stopped. Aghast! Again the metal lid was awry on the crock which sat cooling in the long narrow reservoir the water passed through as it flowed from a vein in the hill.

This time, however, a giant black snake, hung from a beam under the milk house, its head in the cream. The snake had worked its way through a slit between the thick hand-hewn sandstones that formed the sides of the spring. And it had found a place to dine.

Edie had no time to rue her prejudgment of her grandsons. Instead she raced up the hill to a shed, returned with a hoe and separated the snake's head from its body.

She was waiting for Butch, Rusty and their grandfather when they returned from the day's corn planting.

"I have something to show you," she said. She had carried the snake from the spring, its head in one place, its body in another.

Her husband held the snake by its tail. It was more than six feet long, bigger around than his muscled forearms, for it had, after all, been on a cream diet.

Edie apologized to her grandsons and even suggested the next morning that they have an extra bowl of cereal, with all the cream they wanted.

Down in the spring house, a thicker lid, topped with a heavy geode, rested on the crock . . . just in case the snake had left a survivor.

Feed Sack Queen

Nan's mother, her emotions mixed, brought out the new Easter dress she had made.

She was pleased with her work as a seamstress, apprehensive about Nan's reaction to it. "It's your Easter outfit," she told Nan. "Try it on this afternoon so we can make any changes before tomorrow."

Nan didn't bother to hide her disappointment. "I'm 13, going on 14," she said. "I was hoping to get something new from a store for a change."

Her mom nodded, understandingly. "I know. But there's not enough money to buy each of you new shoes, dresses, suits, shirts and everything that goes under them."

"Each of you" meant her other children.

It was the early 1940s and farm families around Heltonville needed what little cash reserves they had for baby chicks, seed and fertilizer.

Nan wasn't comforted. "You know the boys don't care what they wear, anyhow. They'd rather be in faded overalls than in starched collars."

Her mother agreed, but added, "It wouldn't be fair to buy you three girls new clothes and not the boys."

Nan felt the dress with her right thumb and index finger. "It looks nice, but it's made from feed sacks. All the other girls will be showing off new clothes and new shoes with heels. They may look at my dress and call me the feed sack queen."

She reluctantly modeled the dress for her mom, who made some slight alterations.

Nan slumped down as she walked into the rural church the next morning, hoping no one would notice. She was surprised to see that only two or three of her friends had new dresses from stores. The others wore what their mothers, too, had made. She remained disappointed, but relieved, taking comfort in knowing she was not alone.

A few of the older women, who had no children to clothe, seemed proud of their new store-bought Easter outfits, preening themselves, just to make sure others noticed. They were exceptions, and they seldom showed up for services except at Easter.

Farm wives put on no such airs. If they looked around it was to make sure their sons and daughters were well behaved. Most smiled at themselves, happy to see that their teen-agers looked neater, more observant, than on other Sundays.

Nan smiled back at her mom, a signal that she would survive another Easter without a fancy dress from the rack at the J.C. Penney store in Bedford.

She was even more expressive when she arrived home from school a few nights later. She had worn the new dress, and now on her return, she modeled it before the floor length mirror.

"I like being the feed sack queen," she said.

Her mother looked on, curiously.

"Miss P. saw my outfit and said it was about the prettiest looking dress she'd seen this spring. She wants to know if you could make her one," Nan explained.

Miss P. was a stylish young teacher at Heltonville, who knew fashion when she saw it.

Nan's mother made the dress as soon as the mash was emptied from other patterned sacks. Miss P. sent a check in return. The payment was enough to buy a dress at the store, but Nan didn't mention it. She just made sure her feed sack dress was washed so she could wear it again the last day of school.

Happy Ending

Christmas had not been a good time for Belle, and now on the eve of a new year, she seemed even more depressed.

She would not leave home to bid farewell to 1944 or welcome 1945. It would not be for her, or other young wives, a celebration to enjoy.

It had been weeks since the mail carrier out of Heltonville had left a V-Mail letter from her husband. He had written as often as he could, his artillery unit helping the Allies advance across Europe, regaining ground taken by Adolf Hitler's Third Reich.

Victory had seemed imminent at Thanksgiving when the Americans appeared unstoppable as they reached Germany. His letters had been upbeat, optimistic, filled more with the future than the present.

But now there was no mail, no word from him, only newspapers and radio reports filled with grim stories about a setback called "The Battle of the Bulge."

The Germans in mid-December had made a desperate, counter attack along an 80-mile front that reached from Belgium to Luxembourg.

The allies retreated back over the terrain from which they had come. The Germans remained on the offensive for days, driving a wedge 60-miles deep before the campaign sputtered.

The Americans had again taken the initiative, but it would take weeks to regain the ground they had lost.

Belle waited and wondered, searching for any mention of her husband's unit. The battle was too big, too broad, to be covered in detail by newspaper reports and radio broadcasts.

If he had been wounded, it would be days, she knew, before she would be told. Worse news might take even longer.

She tried to dwell on hope, taking encouragement when a Ouija board answered "Yes" when she asked if he was okay, remembered their wedding 15 months earlier near the California base where he had been stationed, thought of the life they had planned together.

She shared her thoughts with other wives who, too, waited and wondered.

And now, Lowell Thomas and H.V. Kaltenborn were reporting the German Army had lost its last desperate chance to change the course of the war.

The battle had been costly, but the Allies were better equipped to sustain the losses, they said in year-end commentaries.

Belle took her thoughts with her, going to her room before midnight, knowing she could not stop the clock or change what the New Year might bring.

* * *

Two weeks or so later the New Year brought a letter in a thin V-Mail envelope with the APO return address. Her husband was well, he had survived the Battle of the Bulge. His unit was no longer the pursued, but the pursuer.

Belle knew the war was far from over, but she sensed, correctly, the future would reveal that the New Year would end a lot brighter than it had begun.

PART XII

"The War Effort"

Youngsters learned from their parents, teachers, other men and women, but it was the war that widened their horizons and took them beyond their isolated worlds.

Newsreels and news stories mentioned names of places they found on maps, places like Pearl Harbor, Bataan, Corregidor, Guam, Wake Island, New Guinea, Guadalcanal in the Pacific. Places like Tobruk, Casablanca and Cairo in North Africa. And places like Palermo, Salerno, Naples, Normandy and Bastogne in Europe.

Generals, Douglas MacArthur, Mark Clark, George Patton and Dwight Eisenhower, became their heroes.

So did young men, brothers and older friends, who were in combat zones. The "Country Bumpkins" wrote letters, sent via V-Mail, letting soldiers and sailors at war know what was going on at home. Tyke and Tad used carbon paper to duplicate news letters and sent them to the most recent APO addresses they had for the men they knew.

Guilt sometimes gnawed at those too young to serve. Some, as soon as they reached 17, enlisted in the Navy, the Army or the Marines. Service would prove to be an education they would not get as high school juniors and seniors.

Those who remained at home, accepted rationing the war had caused, listened to Lowell Thomas nightly, watched news reels when they could.

Mostly, though, they continued to do what teens do. Somehow they knew that was what those at war would have wanted them to do.

Prelude To Disaster

Looking back in the rearview mirror of time, there were few omens of what was ahead those first few days of December, 1941.

Life for most folks around Heltonville continued as usual. Oh, a few men were away at military bases, men like Cladie Bailey, the basketball coach and reserve Army lieutenant who had been activated the previous April. Others had taken jobs at defense plants at Charlestown and Burns City.

But little, on the surface was foreboding, ominous. The weather was too nice for complaints. It had been warm enough to cause apple trees to mistake Indian summer for spring; to bloom, then reach the apple-forming stage in a fatal welcome to a false spring.

Dale Norman, Herman Chambers, Bob Hillenberg, Opal Todd and the rest of the high school basketball team were in class on Thursday, a bit tired after a Wednesday night game at Smithville up in Monroe County. No one razzed them about the 38-28 loss which the Bedford Daily Times called "a rough and tough encounter." All games with Smithville were that way, and the loss by new coach Robert Barrett's team was not unexpected.

And besides, Bruce Temple, a sports writer for the Daily Times predicted Heltonville would defeat rival Shawswick in the Friday night game.

Grade school students looked forward to Saturday afternoon at the Lawrence Theater where they would see Tex Ritter in "Riding the Cherokee Trail" and Bela Lugosi in "Invisible Ghost." High school students made plans to see Edgar Bergen, Charlie McCarthy, Fibber McGee and Molly and a new actress named Lucille Ball in "Look Who's Laughing" at the Indiana.

"Target for Tonight," a war movie "actually filmed under fire," was billed at the Von Ritz.

At grain elevators, wheat was bringing $1.07 a bushel, corn 60 cents, yellow soybeans 1.30, black soybeans 1.06. Hogs were being marketed at $9 to $10 a hundred weight, not a good price, but much better than the $2 of the recent depression years.

Food was plentiful. So were gasoline and tires. Stores offered shoes at bargain prices. Rationing was not yet a household word.

At the general stores, Maine potatoes were 29 cents for 10 pounds, Chippewas 29 cents for 15 pounds. Oranges sold for 19 cents a dozen, bananas 7 cents a pound. Butter was 35 cents a pound, roast pork 19 cents, bacon 25 cents.

Silk hose were advertised "$1 up" at Keller's store in Bedford, where "first quality" men's shirts were $1.49 and men's Oxfords were "$2.98 up." Anyone who really wanted to spiffy up could buy spats for 69 cents.

Travel was unlimited. "Heltonville News" items in the Daily Times mentioned that Earl Todd had driven up from New Albany to visit his parents, Mr. and Mrs. Will Todd. Doyle Lantz, who had played on the basketball team a year earlier, had motored down from his new job at Anderson to spend the weekend with his folks, Mr. and Mrs. Jack Lantz.

The war abroad was barely mentioned, except for a short story headlined, "Nazis Battle Guerrillas in Serb Revolt."

Two recruiters were in Bedford to interview young men interested in joining the Marines, but there was no mention of battles to come. Some men had volunteered for service, but most youths waited to see what developed in those uncertain days.

Their plans—and those of others in Heltonville and elsewhere across the nation—would change dramatically over that weekend to come. Japan would attack Pearl Harbor and the U.S. would be at war.

Time Marches On

For Tad and for his buddies, there was no television. It was, instead, newsreels that brought current news, general interest features and sports events to the screens at the movie houses in Bedford.

"RKO News." "Pathe News." "Time Marches On." Living drama on film that changed from week to week to remain up-to-date.

Tad and his buddies watched—on the newsreels—Joe Di-Maggio hit in his 51st straight game that summer of 1941. And it was on the theater screen that they had seen Ted Williams on his way to a .406 batting average.

The youngsters were interested in sports, less attentive to other news. Oh, they had seen the mad man called Hitler tweak his moustache as his German troops goose stepped across the screen. They had watched Benito Mussolini drive around Rome in his convertible. And they had seen the devastation the Japanese had leveled on China.

But the war in Europe and the Japanese aggression in the Orient seemed far away.

Being teen-agers, they were anxious for the double feature westerns to start. Gene Autry, Roy Rogers, Ken Maynard, Tom Mix were characters to which they could relate. And sidekicks like Smiley Burnette reminded them of some men they knew.

One Saturday changed all that. The boys from around Heltonville were at the Indiana Theater in Bedford. Or, perhaps it was the VonRitz or the Lawrence Theater. No matter. Time may have erased the place, but not the events seen on the screen that day.

It was December 13, 1941, nearly a week after the Japanese attacked Pearl Harbor and brought the United States into World War II.

Tad had seen pictures of the damage in the newspapers. He had listened to teachers who had gone to the packed theater on Thursday to see the first showing of the damage. He had listened as they described the havoc.

He was eager to see for himself, for a boy of 12 visualized war as a mix of glamour and horror. There was no glamour in what he and his friend saw that day, only destruction and devastation.

They viewed the wreckage of the Arizona and heard the death toll, 1,000 plus, more people than lived in Heltonville and

Pleasant Run Township combined. They saw the battleship Nevada in smoke and flames, the damage to the seaplanes on the runway at Ford Island, the burned out bombers at Hickam Air Field.

No one in the theater, lest it be a World War I veteran who had slipped in for the matinee, had seen the terror of war. No one, not Tad, nor his friends, looked away from the screen. No one whispered as he might have done on any other Saturday. The war had become real to them.

Cowboy actors and western shoot outs suddenly became less important, but in the war years ahead movies would continue to be a diversion.

The newsreels would be a visual link to the war, a Saturday update that brought into perspective the stories read in the newspapers and the reports heard over the radio.

Defense Work

Mobilization was a mouthful for most folks around Heltonville. Few adults, certainly almost no youngsters, used multi-syllable words when short ones would do.

There was no point, for example, in saying agriculture when farming was just as descriptive.

Mobilization was no different. It had been used so often on the radio and in the newspapers it became familiar, a word that summarized what was happening as America turned from making products of peace to building weapons of war. But it was seldom used in conversation.

The effort had started slowly back in 1939 after Hitler's war machine had thundered across Poland. The U.S. government had ordered the development of the Charlestown powder plant and the Burns City Powder Storage Depot (later known as Crane).

Reservists were activated and men drafted, but life went on almost as usual for men, women and children around Heltonville.

That had changed on December 7, 1941, a date destined to live in infamy. The Japanese had ravaged Pearl Harbor and soon the nation was involved in the effort to again make the world safe for democracy.

The conversion to war was noticeable, even to 10-12 year old youngsters around town.

Things changed quickly at the Heltonville Limestone Company mill east of town.

Trains no longer crept out of the mill and onto the Milwaukee tracks loaded with stone for skyscrapers in New York and government buildings in Washington. Construction, except for ammunition and munitions plants, came to a standstill.

It was time to convert the mill to defense work. The decision came on February 6, 1942, at a meeting of the owners of the company. They agreed in a short, but significant session to:

* Make every effort to convert the facilities of the company to some phase of defense work.

* Make a survey of the defense industry and take immediate steps to obtain a contract to convert the mill to the production of defense work.

* Declared that only defense work would be considered necessary for the duration of the war.

Within two months, the company had negotiated a contract for the machining of tank parts. That meant an outlay of $50,000 for new machines and another $50,000 to convert equipment already in the mill.

Men who had worked in quarries or had operated diamond saws, gang saws or rip saws, planers and cranes—tools of peace—switched to machines designed to make implements of war.

Car blockers, men who had secured stone slabs on freight trains, now worked with iron and steel.

Men no longer entered the restaurant and general stores in town wearing stone dust. Their careers as stone cutters and stone craftsmen were on hold. They now were defense workers, men helping turn the nation into the world's greatest fighting machine.

They called it defense work. Mobilization was a word for the president, congressmen and commentators.

The Enemy Within

It seemed odd that three characters who resembled Hitler, Mussolini and Tojo would walk into the rural church basement that October evening in 1942.

It was Halloween, however. And the three men who had conspired to rule the world, were at that time the scariest men on the face of the earth.

"Come dressed as you wish," the invitation to the junior high students at Heltonville had said.

The youth leader had anticipated ghosts and goblins, or boys masquerading as Roy Rogers, Gene Autry or Tom Mix, or, perhaps, Captain Marvel. She certainly hadn't expected the Axis leaders to show up.

She wasn't aware, however, of the thoughts that filled the minds of 12-year-olds. Bugsy, Tad and Bogey had debated for days how to dress for the occasion. Once they decided, the rest was easy.

Bugsy, small in stature, light in weight, would be Hideki Tojo, the Japanese military and political leader, prime minister and dictator, who many Americans blamed for the sneak attack on Pearl Harbor the previous December 7.

Bugsy came dressed for the part, a home-styled military uniform, toy sword at his side, poor imitations of Japanese words on the tip of his tongue.

Bogey used his oversized girth to portray Benito Mussolini, fascist dictator of Italy. A belt circled the military jacket his mom had created. A single strap ran from the belt over his right shoulder and down the back, making him resemble the pictures in the news reels shown at the theaters in Bedford. A beret sat atop his tousled hair, accentuating his beefy face.

Tad chose to dress as Hitler. "Adolf" some called him. Others preferred terms like "the Fuhrer" or "that German madman" to describe the "Little Corporal" who had unleashed a blitzkrieg on Europe.

Tad, too, wore a makeshift military uniform. He removed his German style hat as he arrived, exposing hair combed over one eye, raised his right arm, palm out, and shouted "Heil Hitler."

Everyone except Bugsy and Bogey looked at him as if, indeed, he was a German madman, crazy enough to head the Third Reich. That entrance by Tad, Bugsy and Bogey would be the high point of their evening. They were the Axis of the party, men shunned by the rest of the crowd that became allies in disdain of those who dressed as enemies.

The others wanted no part of "Hitler," "Mussolini" or "Tojo." Men of that ilk weren't to be tolerated, even at Halloween. To do so, it seemed, would be to accept them into the brotherhood of the human race, a membership they did not deserve, even in a church setting.

Tad, Bugsy and Bogey left the party early. Each would confess the next day they had hurried home to remove their costumes. Bogey admitted he cleansed himself by taking a bath, even though it was Thursday, not Saturday. They would not be contaminated by the men they sought to portray.

They had learned that in war it's best not to consort with the enemy, not even at Halloween.

Hot Stove Warriors

It was a weekend afternoon in early January 1943 at C. E. Cummings general store in Norman. A cast of characters, farmers with names like Fritz, Eth, Wes, Clyde and Willie, were there. So were their sons, boys called Billy, Bunky, Tad and Tyke.

The men were seated on the benches and chairs around the big stove. The boys leaned on showcases, eating candy bars that were sweeter before sugar was rationed.

The talk—as it had been for a year—was on World War II. The boys didn't talk much when war was discussed. They listened carefully, though, for some of their brothers and neighbors were on duty in the South Pacific, some in North Africa.

Woody, who kept a close watch on the war, entered the store. Tad tried to memorize the conversation:

Fritz: "We've been talking about the fightin' in the Pacific. Heerd anything new?" Heerd was how he pronounced heard, but nobody corrected him for it was character, not speech, by which a man was measured.

Woody: "I tell you boys, it looks like the tide has changed in favor of the good old U.S. of A. and the allies."

Wes: "Hope you're right. It has been a long 13 months since Pearl Harbor and we ain't had much good news since then."

Willie: "We can use some good news, Woody. Tell us about it."

Woody seemed to retain 99.44 percent of what he read and heard. "Well to start with, our bombers pounded Wake Island and plastered them Japs with 75,000 pounds of bombs. Supposed to have been the biggest mass raid of the Pacific war so far. Killed about half the Nips on the island." (In years to come "Nips" and "Japs" would become politically incorrect. But these were men who spoke from the heart, not from protocol or the social registry).

Clyde: "I don't like killings, but it sounds good to me. Go on, go on."

Woody: "Our P-38s led an assault on a Japanese base in New Guinea and shot down nine enemy fighters."

Tad and Bogey applauded and Billy made a sound like a downed Zero going into the water.

Woody: "Don't get too excited, boys. We've got a lot of islands to win back before we get even. Then we got some payin' back to do."

Eth: "Hear anything about what's going on in North Africa?"

Woody: "Not a thing. So I guess no news is good news. The Russians, though are surging ahead on the three fronts in their big offensive against the Germans. And there was a battle between the British and German fleets somewhere in northern waters and the English came out pretty good."

Wes: "The news sure is a lot better than it was a year ago." Everybody nodded.

Tyke: "Well I guess that makes a Happy New Year."

Woody: "No way, boy, can we have a Happy New Year. Not as long as our boys are fighting. We can be grateful the news is better, but let's not celebrate before we got the whole shootin' match won."

A driver pulled up in front of the store, told C. E. to put in four gallons, then complained because he didn't have enough ration stamps to get more. The farmers looked at him with contempt.

Eth said, "You should be happy you're here to drive at all. If you were a couple years younger you might be in a foxhole on an island with some little feller up a tree snipin' at you."

The man paid his bill and left, red of face. The others drifted off into a world still filled with uncertainty.

Life Savers

Chig jumped from the school bus, raced up the hill to the house and bounded the stairs two steps at a time. He changed clothes quickly, tied on his work boots, hurried down to the kitchen, grabbed a cookie and fled, the door slamming behind him.

His mother was surprised. It was unlike Chig. It was the first time that school year he failed to turn on the radio to "Jack Armstrong, the All-American Boy."

On this sunny October day, however, Chig's mind on was on what was called "The War Effort." It was 1944 and Americans, young and old, were united, each in some way involved in helping the armed forces win their battles with the Germans in Europe, the Japanese in the Pacific.

Chig had endured breakfast cereal without sugar, worn old shoes, new ones having been rationed, walked home from basketball practices, gasoline being too limited for his dad to pick him up at Heltonville. If those were hardships, he did not complain. Neither did others, for their burdens were slight compared to those faced by men in battle.

Chig picked up an empty feed sack, crossed a field and walked to a small ditch lined with weeds and briars. And milkweeds. It was the milkweed pods he sought. Each one he gathered would be added to those found by other students at school.

And the Heltonville collection would become a part of the entire Lawrence County output. Chig, like most students, was surprised to have learned milkweed pods could, indirectly, help win the war. His high school teachers had explained that the pods contained kapok, a silky fiber suitable for insulation and padding in life preservers.

Ten pounds of pods were enough for one life jacket.

His sack was about half full when he noticed the sun had set. It was time to do his chores.

He proudly carried the sack over his shoulders onto the bus the next morning. At school, he added it to the pile in a hall. He expected no recognition for patriotism exceeded personal gratification.

It was a week or so later that he learned what he and others had accomplished. O. O. Hall, the Lawrence County school superintendent, announced that students in the county had collected 500 bags, 2,500 pounds, of milkweed pods.

"Our students are responsible for 250 more preservers," Hall said.

Needmore students had turned in 101 bags, twice as many as those at Heltonville. The two schools were rivals in sports, but this had been a competition in which there were no losers. All had joined in "The War Effort."

Chig went back to the radio and "Jack Armstrong" for a few days. Within another week it would be time for him and other students to help sell War Bonds and saving stamps.

Investment In Peace

It was a time of patriotism, a time when Americans had faith in their government and trust in their leaders. It was World War II, a time of war in which there were few, if any, dissenters.

Everyone had a role, be it as a participant, a defense worker, a civil defense volunteer, a food producer or a fund raiser.

Chig and other students at Heltonville were too young to serve, not old enough to work in war plants. They became fund raisers, instead. And in doing so, they learned the virtues of thrift, the yields that result from investments, and the satisfaction that came from being a part of something bigger than themselves.

They had little money. Until the U.S. entered the war against Japan and Germany, they would have spent any dime they had for a Nehi Soda and a Baby Ruth candy bar. No longer! It didn't seem patriotic to Chig to gratify his own desires when some of his teachers and his older brothers were at war. There were more important uses for what money he had.

He couldn't escape the need to help. The two Bedford newspapers reminded him each week, it seemed. Full page ads, which would be labeled "politically incorrect" 50 years later, carried headline such as:

"The job in the Pacific is still terrific?" The text showed a G.I. in a foxhole saying, "There are still millions of tough, brutal Japs to lick. Every Jap we kill makes my chances of getting home better, and it costs plenty to kill a Jap."

The ads, which disclosed that a B-29 bomber cost $600,000 and an M-4 tank $67,417, concluded with another reminder:

"Just as long as a single Japanese aims a gun at our men, we must continue to buy War Bonds."

Chig and his friend could never save enough to buy a war bond outright. But each dime they had would buy a 10-cent stamp that when added to books which when filled could be exchanged for an $18.75 savings bond worth $25 at maturity.

Or if they happened to earn some extra money, they could buy 25-cent, 50-cent, $1 or $5 stamps. Each stamp helped fund the war, as did each pound of aluminum or scrap iron they salvaged.

Saving money became a habit, not only for Chig, but for other students at Heltonville and elsewhere in the county.

Each campaign resulted in increased sales of stamps and bonds. Chig was proud of himself, as were his friends of themselves, when Principal Loren Raines read the results of the sixth War Loan Drive which ended in December, 1944.

Students at Heltonville had bought an even $1,000 in stamps and bonds. Their parents, who lived throughout Pleasant Run Township, had invested another $14,666. If they had depleted the accounts they had saved for Christmas presents, so be it. The best gift would be in knowing, in less than a year, that there was not a single Japanese soldier aiming a gun at an American.

Detasseling Detail

At first glance they may have appeared to be refugees of war. In a way they were.

They were 30 or so teen-agers, some as young as 14, others as old as 17, uncertain about what was ahead. They had arrived in Tipton that July of 1944, riding in a yellow school bus labeled "Marshall Township—Lawrence County," their arms resting on the window ledges, the warm summer breeze in their faces.

They carried clothes in brown paper bags, feed sacks and suitcases secured with binder twine.

Some were from Bedford, city teens unfamiliar with farm work. Others were from rural communities, places like Pinhook, Buddha, Fayetteville, Tunnelton and Heltonville, boys accustomed to field labor.

They had names like "Pig" who was from Fayetteville, "Tommy" of Shawswick, "Nunn" from Williams, "Burge" from Bedford.

All had been recruited to detassel corn in the Pioneer Seed Company's vast fields that spread across the black fertile prairie of Tipton County.

The Bedford Times-Mail had called them the "Victory Team" when they departed. Their efforts, the paper said, would help the U.S.—in a small way—win World War II and bring soldiers home from Europe and the Pacific. They had posed for a photographer, flashing the "V" sign with index and middle fingers, their arms extending from denim shirts with sleeves rolled beyond the elbows.

They did not see themselves as patriots for it was the money that had lured them from the familiarity of home to the apprehension of the unknown. They would make 60 cents an hour from which $1.50 a day would be deducted to pay for their room and board. In Tipton, they soon adapted to their "rooms," bunks in corn bins; meals served cafeteria style in a quonset-type processing plant.

They worked nine, ten sometimes eleven hours, Monday through Friday, until noon on Saturdays, when each was given $2 to spend. The balance would be retained and mailed to their homes once the work was done.

No one quit, lest he face ridicule. There was no way home, anyhow, except to hitchhike. And the company promised a 5-cent hourly bonus for those who chose to stay. Some did complain about the work as they returned from a day in the field, their shirts sweat-soaked, their necks cut with razor-sharp blades of corn. Their disgust soon faded in the excitement of a softball game or a walk down Ind. 28 to a movie in town.

Teens who had met on the bus for the first time became comrades, offsetting each other's homesickness. In four weeks, the detasseling was done, boys had become men.

They stuffed their clothing back into the containers they had brought, climbed on the bus, reducing "Ninety-nine Bottles of Beer on the Wall" to one as the driver rolled through Westfield on U.S. 31 and continued south. Back in Bedford, there was no welcome, no band, no newsmen waiting to greet them.

The teens said farewell, knowing they would see each other again on basketball courts and in pool rooms in the months to come. Some began the walk home, others sought a phone to call their parents.

The Victory Team was home, its assignment completed, its members content with a minor role in what adults called "the war effort."

* * *

Many of the youths would return to Tipton a year later. They would be there when the A-bombs fell on Hiroshima and Nagasaki and brought the war to an end.

EPILOGUE

Once the war ended, life did not return to normal. Lt. Col. Cladie Bailey, a man the "Bumpkins" had hoped would return as coach, had been killed on Luzon in the Philippines.

Charles Kunkel, who had joined the Navy when he reached 17, was lost at sea. Youths who returned had changed, maturing beyond the age of the friends they had left at home.

The "gang" had lost a part of its youth, and its innocence with it. But it dwelled more on the future than the past. It was time to move on with their lives.

Rationing ended, gasoline and tires again were available, and new cars returned to dealer showrooms.

By 1948, most of the "Bumpkins" had graduated from high school. Some would remain in the area to farm or work in factories; a few would attend college and return to teach high school. Some would leave, seldom to return.

Those who had been too young to serve their country in World War II were summoned to duty in the Korean Conflict. They went when called, the age of protest not yet born.

Almost all married, raised families and contributed their time and talents to the communities where they lived. None was ever in serious trouble.

One or two died over the six decades that passed. Those who remain recall the days of their youth each time they meet.